C000246070

One Bloody Afternoon

One Bloody Afternoon

Jeremy Josephs

BLAKE'S
TRUE
CRIME
LIBRARY

Published by Blake Publishing Ltd,
3 Bramber Court, 2 Bramber Road,
London W14 9PB, England

First published in paperback 2000

ISBN 1 85782 406 7

British Library Cataloguing-in-Publication Data:

A catalogue record for this book is
available from the British Library.

Typeset by t2

Printed in Great Britain by
Creative Print and Design (Wales),
Ebbw Vale, Gwent.

1 3 5 7 9 10 8 6 4 2
© Text copyright Jeremy Josephs

Papers used by John Blake Publishing Limited are natural, recyclable
products made from wood grown in sustainable forests. The manufac-
turing processes conform to the environmental regulations of the
country of origin.

Contents

1.
Little Sue

If it came across as patronizing, it was not meant to; it was really a term of endearment. Only one thing was beyond dispute: its accuracy. Whatever the case, the nickname 'Little Sue' was one to which Sue Godfrey had long been accustomed. For the attractive, auburn-haired, thirty-five-year-old mother of two was destined to never quite reach five feet in height.

There were times when that elusive extra inch or two would have been very welcome. But although Little Sue eventually gave up on such dreams, Nellie Fisher could still remember some of the problems posed by her granddaughter's diminutive size: 'I'll never forget how much trouble we had finding shoes small enough to fit her on her wedding day. Or how, even when she was grown up, she was still small enough to sit on her father's knee and put her arms around his neck, to give him a hug.'

Sue Godfrey was always giving hugs. In fact, on the morning of Wednesday, 19 August 1987 she had set out with her two children to give her grandmother an especially warm embrace. For Nellie was ninety-five that day, and gathered at her bungalow in the Wiltshire village of North Newton to celebrate the occasion were Sue's parents, Nellie's granddaughter Joan, and Claire, her greatgranddaughter.

The weather forecast was good: the sun was going to shine for Nellie on this special day. A perfect opportunity, thought Sue, to treat her children, four-year-old Hannah and two-year-old James, to a picnic in the forest on the way. With the children safely strapped in the back of her black Nissan Micra, and picnic and presents packed, she set off to greet the sunshine.

Sue knew how to love. And she too was loved. 'I was so very lucky to get married to her,' explained her husband Brian, 'because I'm the quiet plodder, whereas she was the driving force, so vibrant and full of vitality.'

Brian Godfrey might well be a plodder, but it has not stopped him holding responsible positions as a computer technician for British Airways and later for the electronics group Racal. It was while working for British Airways that Brian was first introduced to Sue, during the summer of 1975, when she was a ward sister at Battle Hospital in Reading. The attraction was immediate and mutual. One year later, with shoes found for the bride, they were wed. It was a big white wedding, with each and every tradition faithfully honoured.

'Sue was always so involved in what I was doing at work,' recalls Brian. 'Leaving for home, if something interesting had happened, I'd think, I must tell Sue that. That's not to say that we didn't have our ups and downs. We did. But everything seemed to be working out as planned. And I remember thinking how good life was.'

That Wednesday Brian Godfrey followed his familiar early morning routine. He left the family's four-bedroomed bungalow in Clay Hill Road, Burghfield Common, a small village just outside Reading. He loved his home and he loved his family. An only child, Brian now basked in the warmth of family life, especially with his wife's large extended family. In fact, old Nellie Fisher boasted well over two dozen great grandchildren, of whom Hannah and James were but two.

'That day I gave Sue a kiss and said, "See you this evening." The kids had come outside and said, "Drive carefully, Daddy," which was always what Sue said.'

Little Sue had been tiny from the start. A premature baby weighing only 2lb 4oz, she owed her life to the medical staff of Battle Hospital, which she later joined as a trainee nurse. She had worked there until 1984, when she left to have her second child. But in giving birth to her son she found herself engaged in a struggle for her very survival. Sue won the fight and little James Godfrey was her prize.

Devoting the greater part of her energy to looking after Hannah and James, Sue was nonetheless able to pursue her chosen profession by working weekends at Reading's BUPA-owned Dunedin Hospital. Mother, wife and healthcare professional, was there time for anything else? Most certainly. Sister Sue, as some people called her, was both extremely active and popular in her village. In fact in August 1987 she was busy taking over the running of the Toddlers' Club, held three days a week in the village hall, and was a force within the local branch of the National Women's Register. She had gone to school locally, and her parents, Ethel and Harold Fisher, still lived in the neighbouring village of Burghfield. Sue was very much a local girl, with Berkshire in her bones. An item in the village newsletter encapsulated her approach to life. Advertising the National Women's Register, it read: 'If you are new to Burghfield, get in touch and make friends. Ring Sue.'

Understandably, Sue had no shortage of friends. That was why she could be sure that the Tupperware party being advertised that week at the local Post Office, and which was due to be held in her home, would be well attended. On Wednesday, 19 August, however, there was just one item on the agenda. Her calendar, packed with summer activities and proudly displayed on her kitchen wall, said it all: 'Keep free. Granny 95. Down Granny's.'

Sue took pride in her personal appearance. For Granny's birthday she was wearing a pretty blue floral dress that seemed to capture the spirit of summer. The children were likewise impeccably turned out, as always, and all the more so on this important day. James sported a Thomas the Tank Engine top, while Hannah wore a pink hairband. Hannah was particularly mature for four, and her mother was in no doubt that her development had been helped enormously by her attendance three days a week at a nursery school.

Not long after setting out, Sue stopped for petrol at an isolated filling station, the Golden Arrow at Froxfield. Mrs Kakoub Dean, the owner's wife, vividly remembers Sue's visit. Not that their exchange was any different from the sort of chat she might have had with a good many other customers. 'But I do remember her saying, "Isn't it a lovely day", and that she also gave me a nice smile,' Mrs Dean explains.

For the picnic, Sue could hardly have chosen a more picturesque spot than the Savernake Forest. Situated near the Wiltshire town of Marlborough, it covers some 6,000 acres, with trees stretching as far as the eye can see, many of them towering birches. Once kings of England hunted there, but nowadays it is better known as the haunt of survival training enthusiasts. For all that, the forest has hardly changed, remaining beautiful, cool and silent.

One Bloody Afternoon

After parking in Grand Avenue, the main road running through the forest, Sue spread out a blue groundsheet and the children's treat began. As young Hannah would later recall, it was while they were picnicking that another car pulled up not far away. It was a D-registration silver grey Vauxhall Astra GTE.

Just before middday, the picnic over, Sue set about packing up with her usual energy and enthusiasm. It would be unforgivable to arrive late at Granny's. Just as she was clearing away the picnic debris, the man who had been sitting in the driver's seat of the Vauxhall got out of his car. It looked like he was making his way towards little Sue.

2.
An English Heaven

'I've lived in Hungerford for almost half a century,' Ron Tarry says with pride. The chubby, grey-haired grandfather has twice been the town's mayor. 'My parents moved here shortly after the war. I was a parachute instructor in the RAF at the time, in India just about at the time of partition teaching Indians how to jump. I've always been very much involved in the town, the community and its organizations.'

Ron's passion has always been football, so it is hardly surprising that he gravitated towards the local club. It was through his interest in the sport that he first came to be involved in public life. Owned by the Charity Commissioners, the Hungerford football club's ground was leased to it by the town council.

'We felt then that we weren't getting a particularly good deal, at least compared to other organizations. So in the late 1960s I got myself elected to the War Memorial Recreation Ground Committee, the people who ran it. The idea was to have our say. Which we did. Then someone suggested that I might run for election to the town council. That was back in May 1972, and I've served on the town council ever since.'

The town council of Hungerford enjoys only parish status, with many of its members being non-party political. Fiercely independent, Ron Tarry fits into this category: 'While I do enjoy the cut and thrust of debate, my sole criterion is always quite simple: is this or that measure going to be good for Hungerford?'

Ron explains how he became mayor: 'I was persuaded to stand as deputy mayor, knowing that I would almost automatically become the next mayor, which, in those days, you could have been for several years. But the then mayor died of a heart attack during his term of office, so I had the office thrust upon me, so to speak. But Joe Brady's widow approached me and said that the next meeting, due to be held a few days after his death, should go ahead. She said that would have been what Joe wanted. So it did go ahead. That was something of a difficult occasion for me. I was elected mayor in 1975, and then for a second year, until 1977, the year of the

Silver Jubilee celebrations. I was therefore mayor for two and a half years, with no thoughts of ever being mayor again. But ten years later, in 1987, I was asked to stand again. Against my better judgement, I was talked into it. My wife, Beryl, was not at all keen. So I said to her that 1977 had been a very hectic year because of the Jubilee. I said that 1987 was bound to be something of a routine year. It wasn't a full-time job anyway. All we had, then, by way of administrative back-up, was a part-time clerk, Mrs Fowler and even she had to come in from Newbury. Anyway, Beryl gave in and I became mayor once again.'

Ron Tarry has something of a reputation in the town for his frenetic energy. When he was not seeing to the affairs of the football club, he would be chairing the town's planning committee, opening a fête or presenting an award. Not surprisingly, this enthusiasm and zest for life, together with his overriding concern for others, combined to make him a well-known figure in Hungerford. Popular and respected, he is devoid of the slightest trace of pomposity or self-importance. The town contains only a few individuals prepared to dart from one meeting to the next, like Ron. For the vast majority, life proceeds at a more leisurely pace.

Hungerford is a picture-postcard market town. Indeed the High Street is coyly, almost self-consciously English and genteel, with its abundant, well-kept deciduous trees, elegant eighteenth-century houses and numerous antique shops.

One Bloody Afternoon

People walk their dogs on the Common; elderly ladies clip their hedges and chat to passers-by; mothers from the choir swap details of how much money they made from last week's coffee morning. On a sunny summer's day the High Street sits wide and sleepy amid the Berkshire Downs. With cars parked nose to the kerb, the market town goes about its business quietly, the only noise coming from a group of ducks squabbling on the banks of the nearby River Kennet.

For some the tranquillity of Hungerford is oppressive, and they move away. But the majority of the town's just over 5,000 residents seem happy to remain, considering themselves more than a little fortunate to have found such an agreeable spot. For many, the trout and grayling fishing on the Kennet proves an irresistible bonus. Here one can well believe, like John O'Gaunt, in a 'Sceptred isle, this other Eden, demi Paradise. This blessed plot, this earth, this England . . .'

John O'Gaunt has long been the town's most famous resident. It was he, the fourth son of Edward III, who, as Duke of Lancaster back in the fourteenth century, had granted commoners' and fishing rights to the people of Hungerford. Since that time the name of Hungerford has been proudly associated with that of John O'Gaunt. There is the John O'Gaunt School, the John O'Gaunt Inn, in fact just about the John O'Gaunt everything. And if the Charter granted by this much-fêted man was lost or misplaced, then the traditions would still be handed down and thus preserved.

To visit Hungerford is to step into history. The ancient borough and manor of Hungerford is governed by the 'Hocktide Jury', consisting of twenty to twenty-four persons selected by lot from among the commoners. Its chief official is the Constable. Since 1458, when John Tuckhill was appointed to that post, the position has been held by nearly 300 people. Other officials are the Portreeve responsible for collecting the quit rents, the Bailiff, three Water Bailiffs, three Overseers of the Port Down, the Ale-testers, the Tithing men, the Town Crier and the Bellman.

Hungerford is rich in tradition. Indeed, many of its traditions are entirely incomprehensible to people from outside the town. This is never more true than on Tutti Day, always held on the Tuesday of the second week after Easter. On Tutti Day the whole of Hungerford goes to town.

'Some people say Tutti Day is all a lot of nonsense,' declares Ron Tarry. 'That it's just an excuse for a big booze-up. But these are an important part of Hungerford's traditions. Because if it wasn't for the work that people had put in in the past to keep their commoners' rights, they simply wouldn't be there now. The Common is now there for everyone to use. And the fishing rights on the Kennet are reserved for commoners or anyone who rents them from the Town and Manor. Tutti Day is the day when the commoners elect all these obscure officials, like our two Ale-testers, whose job is to ensure that the ales are a goodly brew. I enjoy all of these traditions. They are unusual, and very much part of our history. They make Hungerford all the more special.'.

Ron Tarry is right. Tutti Day is certainly unusual. For nowhere else in England are you likely to find two Tithing men, or 'Tutti men', resplendent in morning dress, with beautiful long staves, their Tutti poles topped by an ingenious arrangement of spring flowers and streamers of blue ribbon, being sent on their way by the Constable. And the Constable's orders to his two smart Tutti men? To visit all the commoners' houses to demand a penny and a kiss from all the ladies, even if that means climbing ladders to windows when normal ingress is denied. Maidens are kissed; pennies and oranges thrown to the children.

And so the proceedings continue throughout the day, as they have done throughout the centuries. The Tithing men duly dispatched, the Constable takes the chair at the Manorial Court and the day's activities begin. These include the Hocktide Lunch, which is followed by another Hungerford speciality, 'shoeing the Colts'.

'I haven't really been all that much involved in Tutti Day and the Hocktide Lunch,' Ron explains, 'because these have always been organized by the Town and Manor of Hungerford, whereas my involvement has been more by way of the town council. But I have been invited to the Hocktide Lunch. It's a marvellous occasion. The people attending this lunch for the first time are known as Colts. These people are caught and shoed by the blacksmith, whose solemn duty it is to drive a nail into the sole of the shoe of that person until a cry of "Punch" is heard. When they do this, they then have to pay for a bowl of punch. It really is a lot of fun.'

The term 'Tutti' is derived from the West Country name for a nosegay or a flower, a tutty. With its obscure and ancient rituals, Tutti Day comes but once a year. For the remaining 364 days Hungerford is as it has been since time immemorial. A former resident of the town recalls his childhood thus: 'Of all the quiet, uneventful places in my 1950s childhood, Hungerford was the quietest. I remember those utterly motionless summer afternoons in the High Street. My grandmother and I would get off the coach from London at the Bear Hotel and carry our cases, stopping frequently for rests, up the broad main street, with its redbrick clocktower. Invariably, the town clock would be tolling its slow, flat note, assuring us that, whatever might be happening elsewhere in the world, nothing ever happened in Hungerford.'

In fact something did once happen in Hungerford. For on one of the back roads leading out of the town towards Lambourn there is a monument that few notice. Half buried in the hedgerow, it commemorates two policemen murdered there by a gang of robbers. But that was back in the 1870s, ironically just a few years after the opening of the town's small but proud police station. The former resident was right, though, for ever since that time nothing extraordinary had happened in Hungerford.

For Ron Tarry, Wednesday, 19 August 1987 was a typical working day. He was out and about in his maroon Ford Escort estate, working for his employer, an agricultural co-operative. Ron's task was the same as ever: to sell stock feed, seed, fertilizer and other agricultural products to the farmers of Berkshire.

'I remember that day well,' says Ron. 'The sun was shining. The windows were down. I was driving around the Lambourn Downs, listening to the radio. I was just north of Lambourn at a place called Seven Barrows, and preparing for my next call. Then I heard the early afternoon news.'

3.
'That Shows the Power a Gun Gives You'

Michael Robert Ryan was born at Savernake Hospital on 18 May 1960. His father could hardly get to the registration office quickly enough, and Michael's birth was duly registered in less than twenty-four hours. The reasons for this haste were twofold. First, as a white collar council employee, he knew all about the inner workings of a small local bureaucracy. Secondly, and more importantly, in his mid-fifties Alfred Henry Ryan was delighted to have finally fathered a child. The prompt issue of a birth certificate provided confirmation that Michael Ryan had made his belated entry into the world.

'I remember the day when Dorothy returned from

the hospital with Michael as a baby,' recalls the Ryans' neighbour Guytha Hunt. 'I was thrilled to bits. I saw him grow up from the very beginning. She doted on him, that's the word. I sometimes used to say, jokily so as not to offend, that I wouldn't get him this or that. That I wouldn't jump to it when he clicked his fingers. But she loved him as a son and that was it. There was nothing you could do. It just wasn't up to neighbours like me to interfere. So we didn't.'

Alfred doted on his son too. He was the Clerk of Works for Hungerford Rural District Council, and had a rather unflattering reputation in the area as a perfectionist who enforced strict standards of behaviour. But since he was already approaching retirement when his son was born, he was happy for his wife to take charge of the boy's upbringing. Dorothy, over twenty years younger than her husband, loved her son very much indeed. 'I just don't know what I would do if anything ever happened to Michael,' she would often muse. And the hallmark of Dorothy Ryan's brand of loving was indulgence. Not surprisingly, it did not take young Michael too long to realize that his wishes were usually likely to be fulfilled. Soon the formula had been set: what Michael wanted, Dorothy provided. He became the boy who was given everything: toys and train sets, records and clothes, bikes and, later, cars.

Unlike both her husband and son, however, Dorothy was a well-known figure in Hungerford, and highly respected too. The general manager of the Elcot Park Hotel, where she worked as a part-time waitress for twelve years, remembers his former employee as extremely popular, conscientious and hard working, 'a real salt of the earth figure'. So popular was Dorothy that when, shortly before the summer of 1987, she finally passed her driving test at the twelfth attempt, at the age of sixty-one, the hotel's management presented her with a bottle of champagne, a gesture of admiration for her gritty determination. However, the most constant beneficiary of any additional income generated by Dorothy's dedicated efforts was not herself but her son.

As a young child Michael Ryan developed a particular attachment to Action Man, the commando-style plastic doll beloved of so many boys at that time. True to form, Dorothy saw to it that Michael's Action Man was exceptionally well kitted out, with several different uniforms and virtually every accessory on the market. For this was what Michael had wanted.

'He was moody and self-centred,' his uncle, Stephen Fairbrass, would later recall, 'but that did not mean that it was impossible to like him.' It might not have been impossible, but few did. And when it came to his schooling, Ryan was himself certainly no junior Action Man. Quite the contrary, in fact. He attended the local primary school, just opposite his home in South View, before moving to the John O'Gaunt School. He was a C-stream pupil of below-average ability, as a former classmate recalls: 'He was in a remedial class or in one of the lower sets at secondary school. We used to try to get him to join in games, but he appeared to be moody and sulky, so eventually the other children would just leave him alone. The only person I ever remember seeing him with was his mother, who adopted a very protective attitude towards him.'

As an eleven-year-old, Ryan was photographed along with all the other schoolchildren. Despite the best efforts of the local photographer, even on that occasion he was unable to manage a smile for the camera; indeed it is not difficult to detect a fearful expression on his face. From the very earliest of days, Michael Ryan was a child apart.

Guytha Hunt recalls that throughout Ryan's primary school days she saw little evidence of children coming to and going from his house at South View: 'In fact I never once saw any friend come to play with him throughout those early years. Actually I had a lot of time for Michael, but no one seemed to have a lot of time for him apart from his parents, that is.'

He might not have been seen by Guytha Hunt, but there was eventually one boy, Brian Meikle, who did come to play. He and Ryan were best friends at school, although they eventually grew apart when Brian married in 1980. But during their school years, they were two of a kind, enjoying motorbike scrambling, and both well aware that neither of them was destined to scale the heights of academia. Brian explains: 'Neither of us was very good at school. In the fifth year, when Michael was in a remedial class for one subject, he used to play truant a lot. The other lads used to pick on him because he was small but he didn't get himself into fights because he just wouldn't have been able to stick up for himself. He was certainly no Rambo more of a Bambi really.'

Brian Meikle was right. His friend was frequently a victim of bullying at school. Other children detected his sense of isolation and preyed on it without mercy. And throughout his long, lonely persecution, Ryan would say nothing, preferring to simply take the punishment, always remaining silent and still. His former friend and classmate remembers it well: 'It was quite sad really, because he would always sit on his own. He never did anything to harm anybody. He wasn't popular either with the boys or girls though. He took a lot of stick and it just made him even more withdrawn. He retreated into his guns, and they became his only real friends.'

Nor did Ryan shine in sport. His former physical education teacher, Vic Lardner, remembers only a sullen and shy boy: 'He was quiet, withdrawn you might even say. He certainly wasn't too keen on sports, because it was difficult to get him to take part at all.'

Not surprisingly, Michael Ryan wanted out. The troubled teenager's conclusion could hardly have been more clear: the sooner he was free of the confines of the John O'Gaunt School, the better his world would be. His father, however, was not so eager for him to leave school so soon after his sixteenth birthday, and without a single examination pass under his belt. In the Ryan household a conflict developed as to when and what Michael's next move should be. But when his son promised to enrol at the Newbury College of Further Education, Alfred Ryan relented. Perhaps there, he thought, Michael would receive a more appropriate and vocational type of training.

Having taken his place on the year-long City and Guilds Foundation Course, Ryan seemed at first to have found a home for himself. It was a new and challenging environment. But within a few months a familiar pattern had begun to emerge. For during his time at Newbury College Ryan remained uncommunicative, always attempting to make himself as inconspicuous as possible by sitting near the back of the class. Like many others with whom Ryan came into contact, course tutor Robin Tubb can recall only a shy, repressed personality: 'He was an exceedingly quiet student. He needed a lot of encouragement. He did pay attention though — he was a real trier. It was just that he wasn't very good. I got the feeling that he was frustrated with his inadequacy. He wanted to do well, but he was very timid. If you showed him how to use a chisel, you would have to say: "Now hit it."'

A timid and withdrawn loner, however, was far from the image Michael Ryan was eager to project to the world. For his pattern of behaviour made it clear that his aim was to be taken as something of an Action

Man himself. But a new persona had first to be concocted. He invested in a military camouflage jacket, which, to his mind, lent authority to his idle boast that he was once a member of the 2nd Parachute Regiment. And whether in Hungerford or elsewhere, he would always do his best to walk upright like a soldier, chin up and chest out. Neighbour Victor Noon remembers his antics well: 'Michael was into buying and selling old military swords and he once owned a tommy gun. He was a bit of a military freak and always wore combat gear. He would tend to his guns the way most people would tend to their plants.'

Ryan's shed might have housed a considerable arsenal. He might well have strained to walk upright like a soldier. His patter to the world might have sounded completely plausible. But such boasting and behaviour belonged only to the private world of his imagination. In fact, for Ryan, reality and fantasy were almost equal and exact opposites, as another Hungerfordian, Denis Morley, explains: 'I worked with Ryan together on a project at Littlecote. He was employed as a general labourer there. I thought he was a wimp. He was very much a mummy's boy. She bought him the best motorbike when he was old enough to have a licence. And then he started going round in a posh Ford Escort XR3i. His latest acquisition was a flashy new Vauxhall Astra GTE. He would always have the latest registration plate too. But he certainly wasn't the sort to get involved in a punch-up. In fact he wouldn't even go up a ladder at Littlecote.'

For Ryan, ladders clearly represented an unacceptable risk. And yet he was deeply fascinated by the worlds of survivalism and combat, where the stakes are considerably higher. As a result he was a regular visitor to the Savernake Forest, where several survival huts can be found. Most of these are made from branches broken and woven around a tree in order to blend with the background of the forest. The forest is entrancing, with tangles of pine, beech and oak criss-crossing a network of unmarked lanes, and in season, red puffs of poppies amid the fields of brown, ripening corn which break up the woodland. But Ryan's repeated visits to Savernake were entirely unrelated to the natural beauty of the environment, as Charles Armor, with whom Ryan worked briefly, recalls: 'He used to spend quite a lot of time in Savernake pretending to be on manoeuvres. He used to tell us, when we worked together at Littlecote, that he would camouflage himself and creep up on picnickers without them knowing. He would watch them for a while and then disappear.'

'He were a right nutter, were Michael Ryan. I can remember running around the garden when I was about six years old, some twenty years ago, because he used to use us as moving targets for his air rifle.'

Wynn Pask was right. Ryan had terrorized his younger neighbour for some time. And a good many of Wynn's friends too.

'He never hit us but it was always very frightening,' Wynn recalls. 'Even when he was just thirteen years old, he would lean out of his bedroom window, which looked on to our garden, and take shots at us with his air rifle. It was the same thing when we were playing he would come out with his air rifle. We did complain about it, but not all that much really because we were too scared of him at the time. I often saw him going out into nearby fields and on to the Common with a shotgun when he was just a kid. He even used to take aim at his father's cows, which were kept behind his house. He would shoot at anything, would Ryan. A right bloody lunatic.'

Fourteen years later, Michael Ryan remained gun mad. If anything, his devotion to the world of arms had increased with the years. It was his mother who had initiated him by presenting him with his first gun, an air pistol. Dorothy Ryan was constantly lavishing gifts on Michael, her only child, and the air pistol was followed by a moped, then a scrambler motorbike and, later, a string of smart new cars.

There is nothing to suggest that these later offerings were not appreciated. Yet Michael Ryan savoured nothing so much as the acquisition of a new gun. Whereas supporting the local football club was something of an interest, collecting guns soon became a passion. And wherever Ryan went, his gun went too even if it was just to the local pub for a pint.

Throughout his teenage years and later, Ryan spent long hours tucked away in his garden shed, which soon housed a small arsenal. Every now and then he would emerge to fire at a tin can on the garden fence or take a shot at a bird. The sound of Ryan firing off rounds both behind his parents' house, 4 South View, and in the general vicinity of Hungerford, became quite common.

And then it was back to the garden shed to grease, oil, polish or strip his formidable array of weaponry. Sometimes Ryan's visits to the shed would have no precise purpose, the hours being whiled away simply admiring his treasured collection. Given the opportunity, he could hold forth on every aspect of his hobby for hours, while secreted in his bedroom was a comprehensive range of literature on guns, with books, reviews and survival magazines packing every inch of available space.

Ryan's passion for weaponry singularly failed to impress the next-door neighbours. Just as the Pask family had suffered, so too had the Hunts, who for over twenty years had lived immediately next door to the Ryans at 5 South View. Mrs Hunt remembers Ryan's antics well: 'My husband often used to see Michael coming out of the house with his guns, place them in the boot of his car and then cover them with blankets. My husband would say, "I wonder where he is off to with those guns!" My husband used to keep geese and chickens. And of course Michael was always around and about with his airgun and I remember my husband saying, "Michael, if you kill one of my birds, woe betide you!" He would also go to his bedroom window and shoot the birds in the trees with his guns, and this also upset my husband.'

By the summer of 1987 Ryan's collection of weapons consisted of two rifles and three handguns. They were his pride and joy, something about which he could boast to relatives and acquaintances alike. Nor was there anything illegal in this arsenal kept in the Ryans' brick-built, end-of-terrace council house. On the contrary, Ryan had held a shotgun licence since 1978. As his collection had expanded to include other firearms, so his licence had been amended accordingly, as required by law. The Thames Valley Police had, in the twelve months before August 1987, vetted the young gun enthusiast on at least three occasions, once in November 1986 and twice in early 1987. As the storage facilities were found to be in order, there was no good reason for the relevant authorization to be withheld, and it was not.

Under the terms of his firearms certificate Ryan was entitled to own five guns. It was his constant chopping and changing of his weaponry which had prompted the police visits. Constable Ronald Hoyes, the Hungerford community beat officer, was one such official visitor to the Ryan household. He explains: 'Having worked in Hungerford for thirteen years, I had had no previous dealings with Ryan at all and I knew that he had never been in any trouble with the police, apart from one single speeding offence. He appeared to me to be a fit and responsible person to hold a firearms certificate.'

PC Hoyes's visit was required because Ryan had again applied for a variation to his certificate in order to include a Smith and Wesson, a .38 pistol, for target shooting. The amendment came through without undue delay. Everything was in accordance with the law.

Another police constable, Trevor Wainwright, also a member of the Hungerford Constabulary, took the same view as his colleague on his visits to 4 South View. In fact he lived just around the corner in Macklin Close. These judgements were supported by Ryan's own doctor, Dr Hugh Pihlens, whose name had been associated with Ryan's original application. Again, both PC and GP found Ryan to be sane and safe. Additional legal requirements were duly fulfilled by the purchase and installation of a Chubb steel cabinet, which was then bolted to Ryan's bedroom wall. But in reality the licensee kept the guns and hundreds of rounds of ammunition in the garden shed, a flimsy structure which had long been the nerve centre of Ryan's quasi-military operations, as many neighbours knew.

'Michael was always fascinated by guns,' his aunt, Constance Ryan, confirms. 'It seemed to me as if he felt more important and powerful because of them perhaps because he wasn't all that big himself, I don't really know. But I do remember Michael telling me that once he had met a person while out rabbit shooting and this person had started getting saucy. Michael pulled a revolver out of his pocket and pointed it at the man, and then watched with satisfaction as he ran off. I remember the lesson he drew from this incident very clearly. "That," he said, "shows the power a gun gives you, Auntie." '

Michael Ryan's fixation with weaponry might have made him something of an exception in Hungerford. But he was by no means unusual in terms of the country as a whole. For in the summer of 1987 Britain's gun culture was very widespread indeed. Ryan was just one among 160,000 licensed holders of firearms and 840,000 licensed holders of shotguns. However, the number of shotguns in legitimate circulation at that time was estimated at around three times that number, because several could be held on a single licence. And according to an estimate published in the *Police Review* there were then possibly as many as four million illegally held guns in the country. Gun shops and gun centres were also widespread, with more than two thousand legitimate dealers trading in arms, many extremely successfully, and some eight thousand gun clubs where the enthusiast could hone his skills.

In his love for guns, then, Michael Ryan was not alone. So when he applied to join the Dunmore Shooting Centre at Abingdon in Oxfordshire in September 1986, there was nothing particularly remarkable in his application. For Ryan membership of the Dunmore club was particularly attractive because it incorporated what it claimed was one of the biggest gun shops in the country. Ryan proved to be a good customer, spending £391.50 on a Beretta pistol shortly before Christmas 1986, and then buying a Smith and Wesson for £325, a Browning shotgun, a Bernadelli pistol and two other shotguns during the following year. Ryan borrowed the money to finance these transactions, a Reading finance company handling his repeated applications for funds.

There was more besides to attract the young gun enthusiast, for the Dunmore Centre's shooting gallery had a 25-metre, fullboard, seven-lane range with television monitored targets. The Centre, situated not far from Ryan's home, also had a turning target system, enabling him to practise rapid fire and combat exercises, an area of gun expertise known as practical shooting. Here, accuracy is tested not on Bisley-style targets where closeness to the bull's eye gains the most marks, but under simulated combat conditions, firing at representational figures, usually life-sized depictions of terrorists. The aim here is to kill or maim the 'enemy'. In the summer of 1987 there were no fewer than forty 'survival schools' scattered around Britain, and magazines like *Desert Eagle*, *Combat and Survival*, *Soldier of Fortune* and *Survival Weaponry* were then enjoying a rapidly rising circulation. Michael Ryan was simply one of the gun-loving crowd.

Or was he? Certainly there was something which did not quite ring true. For Ryan's extensive range of macho trappings should surely have made him the envy of the neighbourhood. One might have expected a string of callers at 4 South View:

youngsters anxious to sit in his high-performance car or interested in his impressive armoury. Yet not only was there no waiting list of prospective visitors anxious to inspect Ryan's collection; there was nobody in Hungerford remotely interested in Ryan or his weapons. For the reality was that Michael Ryan's personality simply did not match his image. One of his former workmates, John Mitchell, explains: 'In no way was he ordinary. He had a quiet intensity about him, which nobody really liked. Sometimes he was very pally, but you could tell that the rest of the blokes were not having any of it. He used to talk about how fast he used to drive here, there and everywhere. He was someone you just wanted to stay away from.'

And people did just that. Ryan would therefore occasionally be seen in local pubs standing alone, drinking a pint or two of beer before leaving. Peter Bullock, the landlord of the Red House at Marsh Benham, between Hungerford and Newbury, recalls his surly, solitary presence in his pub: 'I can remember Ryan standing at the bar or sitting at a table. One thing never changed: he was always alone. I don't think that he was a loner by choice, mind you, just that he seemed inadequate.'

Ryan certainly considered his own height of five foot six inadequate. Nor was he very impressed with his head of hair, for he worried a great deal about its premature loss. In fact Ryan was something of a worrier all round, and his doctor was in no doubt that the recurrent lump in his throat which troubled him so was caused simply by nervous stress. His other features were nothing unusual: a beer gut, short light brown hair and a light beard to match.

As a youth Ryan was so reserved and awkward that his headmaster, David Lee, struggles to remember his former pupil: 'He was unremarkable, an anonymous sort of lad really, who failed to distinguish himself either academically or in sports.' Years later a contrived anonymity would continue, with Ryan sporting sunglasses in all weathers, an absence of sunshine not deterring him one iota. Being tough, or being seen to be tough, was certainly important to him. And it was no doubt the feeling of power over youngsters which prompted him once to take a job as a bouncer at local rock concerts. Ryan's new role, with his gun tucked out of sight, neatly matched the image he had developed.

Not surprisingly, Ryan was not much of a hit with women. 'In all the time I knew him,' Gary Devlin recalls, 'I never once saw him with a girlfriend. He was into his guns and kept himself occupied with that.' This is not to imply that Ryan's sexual preference inclined towards men or boys, for it did not. It was just that he was entirely lacking in the social skills which might have led to a sexual relationship. In fact in June 1987 Ryan made such a nuisance of himself at a party by persistently asking a local waitress to go out with him, and refusing to take no for an answer, that he had to be warned off by her friends. And Michael Ryan did not like to be warned off. Not one bit.

By contrast, there was no risk of his being rejected by Blackie, his labrador, whom he loved deeply and looked after very well. Ryan would often be seen out walking Blackie. If anyone crossed his path, or his crossed theirs, then providing that person was not one of the neighbours with whom he had fallen out because of his shooting activities, then invariably his greeting was both courteous and friendly. 'Hello, all right?' he would always ask. Sometimes he would stop and talk knowledgeably to the local children about the latest television film he had seen or video he had hired.

If Michael Ryan was nondescript, so too was his home. The living room was decorated with a heavy, old-fashioned wallpaper of a golden hue. Past the kitchen was a glass lean-to, which his father had built and his mother used as a utility room. Beyond that was the garden, some 200 feet long and complete with a garage and a greenhouse. Michael's room was at the front of the house on the first floor, overlooking the street, which was really a lane, with houses on one side and Hungerford Primary School on the other. This house was the constant backcloth to Michael Ryan's rather dreary and joyless life. It was here that he had been brought, as the only child of his parents, when he was just a few days old.

Dorothy Ryan was a grafter. And invariably she was grafting for her son. She paid for everything: the fast cars, the best clothes and the latest records. She always had, and what is more she was happy to have done so. This suited Michael down to the ground, for while his mother was happy to give, he was happy to take. Her money, however, was hard earned, as she worked as a dinner lady at Hungerford Primary School. The timing of her job enabled Dorothy to have a couple of hours off before starting work again as a silver service waitress at the stylish Elcot Park Hotel at Kintbury, on the outskirts of Hungerford. Here she had felt privileged to serve members of the Royal family on more than one occasion. If guns made Michael happy, therein lay Dorothy's satisfaction too. That explained why she was more than happy to pop across the road every week to pick up her son's pile of survival and gun magazines.

Relatives and friends could see all too clearly that Dorothy Ryan, who, unlike her son, was extremely popular in the neighbourhood, was pampering Michael to a degree which defied description. Michael could be a polite and well-mannered young man, but he was at times a sullen, brooding character, and prone to extreme mood swings. He was often rude and abusive towards his mother. The analysis was hardly complicated: he had been thoroughly spoiled. Aunt Constance Ryan, however, is a little more charitable in her assessment: 'Actually we got on rather well. We shared similar tastes in music and it seemed as if there was not that much of an age difference between us. He was a very, very nice person. But he was also a rather sad and lonely boy. It didn't seem as if he had many friends.'

In 1984, aged eighty-one, Ryan's father, Alfred, had died. It was the end of a long battle against cancer. At first Ryan took the death of his father badly, sinking into a depression, and he turned to his doctor for advice and support. According to Leslie Ryan, his uncle, it was a terrible blow for the young man: 'His father, who he called Buck, was his life. When he went, something in Michael seemed to go too.'

This might have been true in the first stages of Ryan's grief, but it was certainly not for long, according to his cousin, David Fairbrass: 'Michael was quite articulate, but a man of few words. I had known him all of my life and you wouldn't think there was anything strange about him. I only met him with the family, not socially, and he used to drop my auntie down to visit. I never saw his guns, but at his father's funeral he showed me his collection of antique swords. After his father died, Michael became more outgoing if anything. Alfred was quite a disciplinarian, but Michael used to look up to him. Before Alfred's death, Michael was shy, introverted and insecure. But the change that came over him after his father had died was incredible. We could see him coming out of himself. We were all quite pleased for him at the time. And when we heard about Michael's forthcoming marriage we were all very excited indeed. But we never did meet her or hear any name mentioned.'

One Bloody Afternoon

There was a single compelling reason why David Fairbrass was never to meet this fiancée: she was but a figment of his cousin's imagination. Ryan might well have made some progress since the death of his father in terms of the development of his own personality. Yet the fact remained that he was an outsider, a loner, a nobody whose life was so full of rejection and failure that he chose what appeared to him to be a rather satisfactory solution. This was to concoct an altogether more fanciful, successful and dynamic existence which he knew he would never be able to achieve in reality. While his everyday life might have been humdrum, Ryan's fantasy life could hardly have been more colourful.

Witness Ryan's bizarre invention of a relationship with a ninety-five-year-old retired colonel. Mrs Eileen North, Dorothy Ryan's closest friend, recounts the story of this elaborate fiction: 'I worked as a school dinner lady with Dorothy and my own mother lived next door to the Ryan family. I suppose you could say that, relatives apart, I knew the family better than anyone else. Mrs Ryan was devoted to her son and it was she who told people how Michael had become friendly with this colonel who employed a nurse and housekeeper. Michael claimed he was going to fly to India because he had been invited to his tea plantation there, but that the flight had had to be cancelled due to a bad storm. He was also supposed to be paying for flying lessons for Michael. He was supposed to be the owner of a hotel in Eastbourne, although he himself lived in Cold Ash. Not only was he intent on leaving Michael his fortune, he was also due to inherit a five-bedroomed house. Michael also told people that he was engaged to the colonel's nurse, but that the wedding was postponed after she had fallen from a horse. Then the wedding was called off when she refused to buy Mrs Ryan a birthday present. Oh yes, and this colonel person was also meant to be buying Michael a Porsche, Ferrari or Range Rover.'

The story Ryan spun to Edred Gwilliam, a dealer in antique firearms, concerned not an ageing colonel but a young Irish girl. Others were to hear this tale too. Ryan claimed that he had been married to an Irish girl who had borne his child, but that the marriage had run into difficulties after he had caught his wife in bed with an elderly uncle for whom he had once worked. His estranged wife, he told Gwilliam and workmates alike, had returned to Ireland with the child. In any event, Ryan explained, the relationship between the Irish girl and her mother-in-law had always been a troubled one. Ryan's hard luck story had not ended there, for after the death of his father he had been left a lot of money and he and a partner were in business together, renovating properties in London. At one stage, Ryan insisted they had ten or twelve men working for them, but his partner had run away to Australia and left him bankrupt.

Dorothy Ryan had certainly believed her son when he had spoken of the colonel from Cold Ash. It was she, after all, who had picked up the telephone to the Fairbrass family in Calne, twenty-five miles from Hungerford, proudly inviting her relatives to Michael's wedding. Edred Gwilliam had likewise believed his customer, who had, after all, bought a pair of Queen Anne pistols, a holster pistol and an antique naval sword from him over the years and had given him no reason to disbelieve what he said. Nor was there any shortage of additional fantasy. Other tall stories retailed by Ryan included his claims that he had once run a gun shop or antique store in Marlborough; that he had held a private pilot's licence; that he had served with the 2nd Parachute Regiment; and that in 1987 he had taken a trip to Venice on the Orient Express. Every story was devoid of the slightest trace of truth. But wherever Michael Ryan went two things now accompanied him: firearms and fantasies.

Ryan had left school in 1976, just after his sixteenth birthday, without a single qualification. For almost a decade he had drifted aimlessly from one unskilled job to another, with intermittent periods on the dole. He was a great disappointment to his father, who had hoped for better things.

When Ryan did work, however, his style was at least memorable. He once found a job as a handyman at Downe House Girls School in Cold Ash, near Newbury, the town where the fictitious colonel was supposed to have lived. But Fred Haynes, the school's gardener, remembers Ryan's four months' labour there for one reason only: 'He once shot a green woodpecker, which the rest of us found very offensive.'

Between November 1985 and Easter 1986 the gun enthusiast worked as a labourer at nearby Littlecote, the home of the multimillionaire businessman Peter de Savary. Although the great hall at Littlecote was decorated with well over a hundred guns dating from the Civil War, Ryan apparently failed to show any interest in the collection. Littlecote's project director, John Taylor, whose task it was to oversee the £6 million conversion of stately home into historic theme park, remembers Ryan only for being 'terribly over-mothered'. Eddy Pett, also involved in the project, summed up Ryan's personality neatly: 'Michael Ryan seemed a very nice chap to me. He was pleasant enough, but he appeared to be someone who wasn't getting to grips with life.'

Pett was right: nothing seemed to be working out for Ryan. But then things had never really gone his way. The job at Littlecote lasted for only six months, after which Ryan resumed a path that had long been familiar: back to the dole office. Then, in April 1987, after a year out of work, Ryan thought that he might have fallen on his feet. The Manpower Services Commission was advertising for people to work on an environmental improvement project. Sponsoring this programme was Newbury District Council, which appointed John Gregory as the scheme's manager.

One requirement was that applicants had to have been out of work for over a year, a criterion which Ryan was able to fulfil. Ryan knew that the job was poorly paid, at £64 per week, but after a prolonged spell of unemployment he was happy to be back in work. A week after his interview he was working again, this time clearing footpaths and mending fences. At first all seemed to go well and Gregory had no cause to complain: 'Michael Ryan was a good worker, a conscientious worker and he certainly pulled his weight. Although he was very quiet, he was also well spoken and well behaved. I got the impression that he enjoyed working outdoors.'

But Charles Armor got to know Ryan rather better, for he was directly responsible for supervising his work on the project, along with some forty-five other men: 'He was sullen and a bit moody really, but he joined in the conversations with the lads. He would take the mickey out of the chaps, but he did not like it if they took the mickey out of him.'

As ever, Ryan boasted about this or that. And with every statement he forged the inevitable link with the one area in which he seemed to be better equipped and better informed than everyone around him: firearms. Ryan had learned long ago that it was only in the world of guns that he could ever hope to distinguish himself. Not by excelling at shooting for he was just an average shot but through the awesome nature of his chosen field.

When Ryan went to work for Newbury District

Council his pattern of behaviour did not change, for his gun still accompanied him every day. He would turn up for work with his small Beretta pistol tucked between the waistband of his trousers and the small of his back. He also carried a flick knife, and kept another firearm in the glove compartment of his car. It was all for his personal protection, he explained to Charles Armor, and all the relevant paperwork was available for inspection should it be required. But pistols and ammunition had precious little to do with fixing footpaths and fences, as Armor emphasized to Ryan: 'I told him to his face that he had no right to carry guns. I said that a licence didn't mean that he could carry loaded guns. So I felt it was my duty to report him to Mr Gregory.'

Once, while working on a project in Calcot, Ryan embarked on a familiar refrain, boasting to his workmates that he could get them any gun they wanted. In fact, he said, he could get hold of almost any type of military equipment they might have cared to choose. And for sale on the spot, no questions asked, he had a box full of flick knives, which he was offering for the very reasonable price of just £5 each. Next to these knives, in the boot of his car, would be an assortment of shotguns and rifles. He even brought his homemade bombs — Ryan Specials he used to call them — and rockets to work, and one day decided to demonstrate one of the latter while working by the Thames at Reading.

'It nearly gave me a heart attack,' Charles Armor

recalls. 'It went up in the air, came down and took off again straight towards some houses. I shut my eyes. It scared the living daylights out of me, but then it dropped down to the ground.'

Were Ryan's activities just harmless fun? The antics of an over-enthusiastic amateur? Not according to Armor. Because once, after Ryan had suffered a particularly harsh ribbing from two fellow workers, he lost his temper in a rather spectacular way. 'He said he would shoot them if they didn't leave him alone,' Armor explains. 'He was serious about it. He was gritting his teeth in temper. I could see what was coming and I told them to leave him alone.'

Ryan also boasted of clandestine nocturnal expeditions during which he would use road signs for target practice. At first Armor refused to believe Ryan. But after his recent rocket display Ryan's supervisor was not too sure what to believe. It was only when he went to inspect a signpost on the Shefford Road to which Ryan had directed him, that he realized that he had been serious after all. For there he witnessed a road sign peppered with four bullet holes. Armor knew that he now had to act, for the time had come for Ryan to go.

Ryan pre-empted Armor's disciplinary measures, however, by walking out of his job on 9 July 1987. His departure was true to form, for he left claiming that he had found a better job with better pay. In reality he went straight back on the dole, where he could claim £54 a week, just £10 less than his weekly wage. Unemployment conferred on Ryan one major advantage: he could now devote himself entirely to shooting. He had hardly visited the Dunmore Centre in recent months; but now that situation could be redressed. Ryan might not have been getting to grips with life, but he certainly knew how to handle a gun. Here was where his heart had always been, with firearms, not fences. He now had some serious shooting to do.

Within four days Ryan had joined another gun club. This time it was the small, privately owned Tunnel Rifle and Pistol Club, based in a disused railway tunnel in Devizes, Wiltshire. The club had over 600 members, at least thirty of them policemen, and was extremely well run. Probationary membership number R62287 was issued in return for Ryan's £50 joining fee, which he paid for with his Barclaycard. Once again, for those whose job it was to vet prospective applicants, Ryan cut a very credible and even respectable figure. Andrew Barnard, a partner in the Tunnel Club, certainly harboured no doubts about his eager new recruit: 'He was a very unremarkable sort of person. He was polite, very safe on the range, and never did anything to give us the slightest worry. He seemed to me to be a typical country person. He came over as perfectly bright and gave the impression of being well educated. The only military gear which he ever wore was a pair of Dutch paratrooper's boots, which were always well polished. Otherwise he was always smartly dressed. He would have looked quite good with the green welly brigade.'

A few weeks earlier, while he had been traumatizing Charles Armor on the Manpower Services Commission project, Ryan had applied to the Thames Valley Police for yet another alteration to his firearms certificate. Apparently there had been a qualitative change in the type of weapon he craved, for now he sought permission to own two 7.62mm self-loading rifles. Ryan's pistols and self-loading rifles were known as Section I weapons under the 1968 Firearms Act, as opposed to Section II weapons, which are shotguns. And in order to obtain a certificate for Section I guns, an applicant must first satisfy his local police authority that he is a fit person with a legitimate reason for their possession. Once again, Ryan was able to satisfy the Thames Valley Police, although he was not yet a full member of a club that had proper facilities for these weapons. He enjoyed only probationary status at the Devizes centre, whereas his Abingdon club, where he did now have full membership, did not at that time have approved facilities for such weapons.

With his newly varied certificate, Ryan knew that he was legitimately entitled to buy weapons of an altogether greater menace, which was precisely why he had applied for the change. Having obtained it, he could not get to the gun shops quickly enough. Their staff now had no reason to deny him his prize.

On 15 July 1987 Ryan travelled to the pretty Wiltshire market town of Westbury, where he made for Westbury Guns, situated at 12 Edward Street. The shop's presentation was typically 'county', with stuffed vermin and books such as *Shooting Made Easy* in its olde worlde windows. Nigel Shimwell greeted Ryan. It was not the first time they had met. Before long a £310 transaction had been agreed. Ryan produced his credit card once again, and paid a £50 deposit, and then pulled out his firearms certificate and driving licence. This was sufficient documentation to persuade the gun dealer to allow Ryan to pay off the balance, with interest, over a period of months.

The upshot of the deal was that Ryan returned to his car with a Chinese 'Norinco' version of the famous Russian semi-automatic Kalashnikov AK47 assault rifle tucked under his arm. This weapon, known as the 'widowmaker' by the IRA, and favoured by terrorists all over the world, is extremely powerful, and capable of firing thirty times faster than a finger can pull the trigger, with each magazine holding thirty rounds.

Despite the terrifying nature of the rifle's firepower, during the summer of 1987 thousands of AK47s were available over the counter and by mail order in Britain at bargain basement prices. In fact, had Ryan shopped around, he could have obtained the identical weapon for £50 less. It was on sale to anyone with a firearms certificate for a standard 7.62mm target, and more often than not, credit was readily available too. The certificate itself cost just £12.

When Shimwell sold Ryan his new weapon, however, he did so without trepidation. Because in the world of gun enthusiasts there was nothing unusual about the direction in which Ryan's hobby had taken him. Indeed, hundreds, if not thousands, of Kalashnikovs were then in private hands in Britain. Ryan could hardly wait to try out his new semi-automatic. On 23 July, and again on 26 July, he used it on the club's ranges, aligning the sight. He was now practising virtually every other day: it was as if he was in training for a particular event.

Unlike Ryan, many of the members of the Tunnel Club were pillars of the Establishment. One such member was Gerald Sidney, a Somerset and Avon magistrate. He remembers his meeting with Ryan well: 'He was sitting in a chair at the top end of the rifle gallery. He had just finished firing off a magazine from his Kalashnikov. I had never seen him before. I said hello and he replied that he had just been zeroing in his new rifle. The gun seemed in very good nick. The trouble was, when we looked at his targets, his shooting was all over the place. It looked to me as if he wasn't that good a shot.'

All the more reason, then, for Ryan to improve his technique. On 2, 4 and 6 August he was back at the club, sparing no expense for the 7.62mm cartridges which his new weapon was consuming so greedily. In fact he was so thrilled with his new acquisition that he decided the time was ripe to invest in another rifle. So it was that on 8 August he paid £150 for a US Second

World War M1 carbine, and spent an additional £17 on fifty rounds of ammunition. The weapon was purchased at the Devizes club itself, from Andrew White, the co-owner, Ryan again proffering his Barclaycard. To Andrew White there appeared to be little cause for concern. Nor was he the first to have taken this view.

'Michael Ryan was unusually safety conscious,' White explains. 'I should know because I sold him the M1.30 carbine and taught him how to use it. I could tell by the way he talked that he knew all about their history. He visited the club about a dozen times altogether and he was always rather polite. In fact he would usually have a chat and a few laughs when he came into our shop. I found him to be a very good shot for someone of his experience. He hit an 18in x 14in target consistently at 100 metres. I had no doubts whatsoever about selling him the carbine. It's a very popular rifle and very compact.'

Two days later Ryan was again back at the club working on his shot, and again two days after that, when he invested in an additional box of .30 cartridges for the carbine. Ryan's licence now entitled him to legitimately hold the following weapons: a 9mm Beretta pistol, a .22 Bernadelli pistol, a .32 CZ pistol, a .30 Underwood carbine and a 7.62mm Kalashnikov rifle. Under the terms of his licence he was also permitted to hold as many shotguns as he required. Although Ryan's collection had by now acquired a distinctly military character, his neighbours were nonetheless unable to detect any change in his behaviour. He appeared to be his old self, a solitary figure always out walking his dog, yet invariably willing to pass the time of day with passing neighbours.

On 18 August Ryan paid a final visit to the Tunnel Club. Andrew White explains: 'He phoned in the morning and said could he come and shoot at two in the afternoon. He shot for one hour, paid his range fee of £1.70 and used two targets. There were no problems whatsoever and he just left the range saying cheerfully, "See you about, cheerio." But I did notice a bit of a change in his personality on that Tuesday. He was rubbing two pound coins together in his hand, fidgeting with them between his fingers. There was none of the usual chatting or joking about.'

If Andrew White thought that on 18 August Ryan appeared a little edgy, Colonel George Styles was also on edge. This nervousness was entirely attributable to his meeting with Ryan the day before. Colonel Styles, also a member of the Devizes club, was formerly the army's chief firearms expert in Northern Ireland. He also found Ryan to be a well-presented young man in full possession of his faculties. And yet the former soldier came away from his meeting with Ryan with alarm bells ringing in his ears: 'When I met Ryan on that Monday he was speaking to Andrew White, one of the directors of the club, and holding his AK47 rifle. I started to think that this fellow must be a very, very important person to have got permission for a

Kalashnikov. Perhaps he was a member of the Special Forces, or the police. Or in the England shooting team. I wasn't really sure. But he wouldn't have got permission for it if he was just an ordinary young man. We talked about the cleaning, stripping and maintaining of the Kalashnikov for about ten minutes, during which I whipped the top cover off the gun. But when I gave him the cover he couldn't even get that back on. I thought, how on earth was he allowed to buy this gun when he doesn't even know how to use it and he can't even get the cover back on?'

Colonel Styles might well have been one of the country's leading firearms experts, but his assumptions about Ryan's shooting credentials were wildly inaccurate. Ryan was not a member of the Special Forces. Or if he was, it was only in his fantasies. He was not a member of the police, though he would no doubt have found their Tactical Firearms Team of particular interest. And he was certainly not in the England shooting team. Still, the acid test remained whether or not these potentially lethal weapons were likely to be abused. The Thames Valley Police had long ago made up their minds. Their main concern had not changed over the years: that such a weapon should not end up in the wrong hands.

Whatever his other peculiarities, Ryan had always been responsible about his firearms. Nor was his interest merely a fad. Indeed, one could not help but admire him when it came to his attitude towards his dying father. For then his sense of correctness about his weaponry had surely shone out. Two years earlier Alfred Ryan had been losing his battle against lung cancer. Crippled with illness and riddled with pain, he was eventually confined to a wheelchair. Aware that his days were numbered, Ryan senior asked his son for some assistance in bringing about his end, in giving nature a helping hand. His request was simple and direct: would Michael please leave one of his guns at his bedside, loaded with a single bullet?

'No,' Ryan replied sternly. 'No. Certainly not. Guns aren't meant for killing.'

4.
A Peaceloving Man

PC Roger Brereton did not share Michael Ryan's enthusiasm for the world of weaponry. Quite the opposite. For during the early part of August 1987, he and a colleague from Newbury police station had been discussing the issue of arming the police. Both had agreed that the British 'bobby' was able to police more effectively precisely because he was known to be unarmed. The point was for policing to be, and to be seen to be, by consent, not compulsion. So strongly did the pair believe in an unarmed police force that they both resolved to tender their resignations rather than be obliged by law to carry guns.

'I met Roger at a coffee bar in Reading back in

1964,' Liz Brereton recalls. 'It was at a place called "The Thing". Actually the bar was more of a nightclub really. I can remember our meeting very clearly, because Roger tripped over me. It was during the evening and quite dark. I had been sitting on the floor — there were no seats, this was the Swinging Sixties, remember — when this person stumbled over me. I looked up and thought, he's cute and that was it. I just knew as soon as I looked up that he was the one for me. On my part it was very much love at first sight. I knew the friend who he was with, and he introduced us. Roger then went up to the jukebox, put a record on and asked me for a dance. And that was it. I was a mod then, and so was Roger. He was looking great in his parka, with fur all around the hood, while I was dressed as a mod too, decked out with my suede coat. That coat went everywhere with me, even in a heatwave. I was probably in ray bell-bottoms too. We were both just eighteen years old.'

That night Roger Brereton asked if he could escort his new mod girlfriend home. Almost immediately, Liz could see that there were a number of formidable obstacles to be overcome if their romance, scarcely off the ground, was ever going to succeed. She explains: 'As soon as Roger told me that he was in the Navy, I knew that things were not going to be easy. He just happened to be home on weekend leave when we met. His rank was LREM — leading radio electric mechanic. I have always had a bit of a thing about men in uniforms. But to be honest it wouldn't have mattered what he was wearing, because I just knew that he was for me. Anyway, that night he told me that in about twelve weeks' time he was off to Mauritius for eighteen months. I thought, right, that's it, this relationship doesn't stand a chance. I said to myself that I wouldn't be seeing him again — because you know what they say about sailors.'

Whatever it is they say about sailors clearly did not apply to Roger Brereton. Because within a few days Liz had received a postcard from Nairobi, where he had changed planes. The following week a letter arrived, and they continued to arrive throughout the eighteen months of their separation. His commitment was as strong as hers. Nonetheless, it was a courtship of correspondence and all the more difficult because of that.

'Well, those eighteen months did go by. Eventually he surprised me by just turning up at the office where I was working. Downstairs reception called me. My legs were like jelly when I saw him again for the first time. His back was towards me, and as I walked from the stairs to where he was standing, it was the longest walk in my life. I greeted him with the words: "God, you've put on weight!" But after an hour chatting together it was as if he had not been away.'

Within a week they were engaged to be married. There were to be more separations, though none as long as the Mauritius trip. In 1968, after a four-year courtship, they were wed — only for Roger to be sent off to sea again shortly before their first wedding anniversary, by which time Liz was seven months pregnant. When Roger returned after a year, he set his eyes for the first time on Shaun, his bouncing, ten-month-old son.

'That was terrible for me, I must say,' recalls Liz. 'I had a telegram at the hospital and that was it. I used to have a particularly hard time in the evenings, when all the husbands would come to visit — except mine. But everyone used to make a fuss of me and that did help a bit.'

A year and a half later Paul Brereton was born. After eleven years in the Navy, Roger was reluctant to leave his young family any more. Instead of becoming easier, the separations had become more difficult to endure for Liz and Roger alike. Committing himself to a second eleven-year term was simply unthinkable.

Roger had made up his mind to join the police. In many respects, it was a logical move. He had thought of such a career as a schoolboy, and what he really wanted was to be a traffic cop.

'Of course, I knew that there was a certain amount of danger in Roger joining the police force,' Liz reveals. 'But he would have gone mad just doing an ordinary nine to fiver. There is always this underlying tension in the police force, this fear that something might happen. One way of coping was for we police wives to be very supportive of one another, which we were. Because it was the same for all of us. HQ were always very good too, often ringing up, at Roger's request, if he was going to be late. But it was still always very nice to hear the key in the door.'

A sensitive man, PC Brereton would often try to allay his wife's fears. His standard light-hearted line was to the effect that should any maniac happen to strike in the vicinity, he would be the first person, and the fastest, running in the opposite direction. It didn't help a great deal, but just to address the family's worst fears could itself be therapeutic.

Roger Brereton began his police career as a bobby on the beat in Wantage, in Berkshire. The Breretons first lived with his parents, then hers. The new police constable would walk or cycle around his beat and soon developed a local reputation as a popular and friendly policeman.

'I was proud of him being a policeman. At least I could see him every day or night, according to which shift he was working. And I knew that once the initial training period at Hendon was out of the way, then there would be no more separations. He went on the driving course, passed it — and then waited for a posting. It was Newbury. When he passed the driving course, he was over the moon — you couldn't get his head through the door. And I do remember thinking when he became a traffic cop, thank God for that — now he'll only be dealing with TAs — traffic accidents, that is. That now he would be safe.'

Brereton loved his work. His childhood dream had come true. There were indeed lots of chases, accidents and 'domestics'. The work was always interesting and varied. Seldom was there a shortage of compelling anecdotal material to retail to Liz. For policing purposes Brereton's Newbury traffic base had within its jurisdiction the town of Hungerford. The two towns also had other links, for radio communication at Hungerford was by way of personal UHF radios operated from Newbury, and Hungerford was in any case part of the Newbury Sub Division, and its personal radios were controlled by the Newbury Control Room.

Professionally, Brereton had little to do with Hungerford, however. When the Breretons set foot in the town it was more likely to be for pleasure than police duties, for both were very fond of the place. A favourite treat was to picnic on the Common, or to browse around the parade of antique shops, second to none in the area. Only ten miles from their police house just outside Newbury, for them Hungerford was the ideal outing.

Roger Brereton was certainly a friendly man, but he could also be tough. How else could he have broken up a pub brawl in which knives were used, as he had once had to do? But he was aware that as far as the implementation of the Road Traffic Act was concerned, sometimes a severe dressing down could be just as effective as an endorsement or a fine. He once decided to adopt such an approach with a motorist who was driving at well over the speed limit on the M4. As he launched into his reprimand Brereton could not understand why the motorist was not suitably humbled, or what might account for a smirk on his face. Being caught by the police driving at over eighty miles per hour on one of Britain's main motorways was surely no laughing matter. Brereton had failed to remove some Christmas decorations from his policeman's hat after the annual office party, and it was the juxtaposition of tinsel and a ticking off which had proved so comic. Always keeping a keen eye on those with designs on the speed limit, Brereton had also once stopped a member of the Royal family for this same offence.

On the morning of 19 August 1987 the sun was shining and there was a gentle breeze in the air. At eight o'clock Roger Brereton set off for work. Liz was showering when he rushed in to kiss her goodbye. Both had overslept and there had been a rather unseemly rush for the bathroom.

'It wasn't much of a kiss really,' Liz explains. 'His glasses steamed up as he popped his head round the curtain. I reminded him that he had forgotten to wash his hair, because he always liked to look his best for work. As he rushed down the stairs he shouted out: "Not to worry, I'll do it tonight. See you later."'

Liz topped up the family income by working as a home help. She would tidy the homes of the elderly and infirm, cheering them up in the process. Because a police career is so finely structured, both in terms of age limits and pension rights, many personnel and their families begin to address the issue of retirement relatively early. Roger Brereton was no exception. He always liked to think ahead. In his own mind, at least, his agenda was very nearly fixed. He would in time buy a pub and retire to the West Country. Roger and Liz would run it jointly, and for both it was a very appealing prospect. Occasionally, as Liz went about her work, she would permit her mind to embroider this scenario. Every time, she liked very much what she saw.

But that Wednesday has stayed in her mind for a very different reason, as she explains: 'Normally, when I used to go on my rounds as a home help, most of the houses I went to would have their radios or televisions on. But on that Wednesday none of them did. When I got to my last lady, it was ten to one in the afternoon, and I could hear the sound of police sirens. I knew I would hear all about it later that evening when Roger would get in from work. I thought it was probably a bad TA. In fact I can remember my exact words to that lady: "Some poor bugger's in trouble," I said.'

5.
'Something about that Michael Ryan'

If, on that sunny August morning in 1987 when Sue Godfrey and her children were picnicking in the Savernake Forest, Michael Ryan was behaving strangely near by, so too had he been doing at home. Towards the end of July he had become involved in a row with Mrs Christine Reagan, a neighbour whose children had been irritating him by playing on his drive. Ryan's remedy for any such minor trespasses was to fire airgun pellets at his neighbour while she was hanging out her washing. A little earlier in the year he had also crossed swords, almost literally, with another neighbour, Ivor Pask, on whom he had threatened to draw a knife after an argument prompted by the constant fouling of the footpath by Ryan's dog. Others within the vicinity had come to fear Ryan too, most notably the children of South View, who had long been terrified by his style of driving as he roared off on his solitary evening excursions in his sporty Vauxhall. Justin Mildenhall recalls: 'He was mad in his car. Our alley's so narrow, there's no footpath. So if a person in a car comes up and there's someone in the lane, they normally slow past on the bank. But Michael, he'd just go up there really fast, and you would have to press yourself against the hedge or be run down.'

While Ryan was sporadically terrorizing his neighbours, a tragedy was unfolding on the other side of the globe. For on 9 August 1987 the quiet of a Melbourne suburb was shattered by a young man named Julian Knight, a nineteen-year-old failed army officer cadet. He had kitted himself out in paramilitary gear and armed himself with two semi-automatic rifles and a shotgun. He then stalked passers-by from behind bushes, picking them off one by one. In this way he casually murdered six people and wounded a further eighteen. The drunken gunman was finally caught by a wounded traffic policeman, but only after he had run out of ammunition.

But why should a person explode in such a destructive and murderous fashion? For decades psychiatrists have struggled to provide compelling explanations. And yet the personalities of inexplicably

violent offenders have been documented nonetheless.
For, as long ago as 1963, a group of doctors published
a paper entitled *The Sudden Murderer*, which can be
found in Britain's Archives of General Psychiatry.

'Such a murderer,' they argued, 'was likely to be a
young adult male, with no history of previous serious
aggressive anti-social acts, who had been reared by a
dominant natural mother in a family of origin that
had been overtly cohesive during the patient's childhood. The father had either been hostile, rejecting,
overstrict or indifferent.'

Building on this research, Jack Levin, Professor of
Sociology at North-eastern University, Boston, has
been able to construct a model for the type of person
who, like the gunman Julian Knight, kills
indiscriminately. There is a combination, according to
Levin, of frustration, a precipitating event such as
unemployment or divorce and, most important of all,
access to and training in firearms.

The problem with such a model, however, is that
large numbers of people can fall within its scope.
Certainly many millions of people are frustrated with
various aspects of their lives. Millions divorce.
Millions are unemployed. And certainly large
numbers of people have both access to and training in
firearms.

There was indeed something distinctly odd about
the behaviour of Michael Ryan; a good many of the
people of Hungerford could have testified to that.
Furthermore, he fitted Levin's model. But then so did

59

many other members of the Tunnel Rifle and Pistol Club. And when Peter Browning, then a thirty-five-year-old Royal Marine, met Ryan at the Devizes club on the afternoon of Tuesday, 18 August, nine days after the carnage inflicted in Australia, he was quite unaware of the slightest trace of abnormal behaviour: 'I remember that he was wearing brown paramilitary boots, a pair of plain green denim fatigue trousers, a green woolly jumper and a shooting duvet jacket. To me he looked like a regular gun club member. He was really very polite. Just a nice pleasant lad who liked to talk to people about guns.'

A number of Ryan's neighbours from South View knew otherwise; so did various colleagues from his last foray into the world of work. But ask them to be more specific and they would be at a loss to identify with any precision what it was about Michael Ryan that set him apart from the rest. Even Ethel Stockwell, a retired nurse and a close friend of Dorothy Ryan, never fathomed Ryan's personality: 'I don't know what it was about that young man. He was impenetrable. But there was definitely something about him. Yes, there was definitely something about that Michael Ryan. And yet I could never quite manage to put my finger on what it was.'

6.
Tactical Decisions

There was nothing strange about Paul Brightwell. His career had followed a conventional enough path. He had joined the Thames Valley Police in 1970, and served at a number of its centres, including Aylesbury, Slough and High Wycombe. For many years he had worked in the Traffic Department. But with a view to advancing his career and adding spice to his daily routine, he eventually applied to join the Support Group, whose officers constitute the Tactical Firearms Team.

'I was in the Support Group between 1979 and 1985,' Brightwell explains, 'when I was promoted to the rank of Sergeant. I then left for a couple of years only to return to the group as a Sergeant at the beginning of 1987. I was then thirty-five years old. When I married Sandy I was already in the job, so she had a fair idea of the sort of work I would be involved in and she has always backed me all the way. I do enjoy our rather specialized field of work. Mind you, I also find the whole area of firearms rather difficult. Because, unlike many people in the group, I'm not a natural shot — just a good average — so I really do have to work at it.'

The first Thames Valley Police Support Group began operations in 1969 on an experimental basis under the command of the Assistant Chief Constable. It consisted of twenty-seven selected officers and dog handlers. The object of the Group was to provide a highly mobile unit of officers, able to perform a preventative role, to support divisions in most aspects of police work and, perhaps most important of all, to give immediate assistance after a report of a serious crime.

In its early days the Group was most active in and around Aylesbury, Amersham, Slough, Bracknell and Reading — familiar terrain to Sergeant Brightwell where crime was rife. But it also assisted both in large scale enquiries and local events such as the Henley Regatta and Royal Ascot.

By 1970 an independent streamlined unit was in place, with a remit covering the whole of the Thames Valley police area. As the years went by, so the Support Group grew in both stature and reputation.

Nonetheless it still retains its initial role, continuing to deal with a variety of incidents, such as the policing of major events, crime investigations, house to house enquiries, searches and preventative patrols in response to terrorist threats.

The major function of the Support Group, however, is that its officers form the Thames Valley Police's Tactical Firearms Team, and this has always been the cornerstone of its role. The Team is specifically trained to conclude armed incidents, whether confronting a gunman on the loose or attempting to conclude a siege. It is a highly trained and heavily armed specialist squad whose overriding duty is to provide an efficient, disciplined, twenty-four hour response to any shooting incident within its police area. Considerable skill and experience are required of candidates for the Group, and every officer selected is trained to a high degree in both tactical and shooting skills.

The Support Group now consists of forty-eight officers headed by a Chief Inspector. There are two Inspectors, one with responsibility for the north of the police area, the other mandated to cover the south. Under each Inspector there are two parties of ten constables and a sergeant working alternate day and night shifts, with one constable acting as co-ordinator. The precise nature of the work of the Support Group remains shrouded in secrecy, and it uses unmarked vehicles, although these are equipped with portable blue lights and two-tone horns or sirens.

During the summer of 1987 the head of the Support Group was Chief Inspector Glyn Lambert. Having had an operational career within the Thames Valley Police, he had been selected first as an Inspector in the Support Group, before going on to head it. Chief Inspector Lambert describes his role and the work of the Group thus: 'Of course I have passed all the necessary firearms courses myself. But you need to be more than just a proficient shot: you must be able to think and to train tactically. You have to learn how to move around and to be sensible in your approach. Whenever a major firearms incident occurs within our jurisdiction, overall control actually falls to the Assistant Chief Constable. But because of my advisory role as the tactical firearms officer my role is also quite crucial, with my advice being sought on the firearms issue. Once notified of an incident I will ensure that our firearms package gets rolling — that is to say, the communications package, tactical dogs, weapons, officers, helicopters and whatever else I think might be helpful and relevant for the operation. Of course we do have powerful rifles in our pack, although I have to say that the Kalashnikov is a hell of a weapon. That's because it's self-loading. Once launched, its bullets travel at 2,900 feet per second — and they can cover a distance of up to four miles. And because of its high penetration, it really is a most fearsome weapon.'

Chief Inspector Lambert indeed had a highly trained group of men, but he did not have the most modern equipment. For example, the control room at the force's headquarters at Kidlington had out-of-date communications equipment. Nor at that time did the Thames Valley Police then have their own armoured Land Rovers. At the time of the Hungerford massacre, these were a new thing for the police. While the Metropolitan Police had some, few other forces did, and in any case they were not often needed. Compared with some forces in the country, however, the Thames Valley Police were privileged, as Chief Inspector Lambert explains: 'In 1987 there were only four police helicopters in the country. And we were fortunate enough to have one at our disposal. I always have great faith in the helicopter and I like to work closely with it because it really is an excellent spotting tool. On Wednesday, 19 August, however, it is true to say that our helicopter had been temporarily grounded for repairs.'

While repairs were being carried out on the helicopter, the officers of the Support Group were at Otmoor, an army training range, where they had gone to meet the Firearms Training Unit. Sergeant Paul Brightwell was there on that day, and recalls: 'That Wednesday had been allocated as a firearms training day at Otmoor, which is about eight miles north of Kidlington HQ and therefore not so far from Oxford. Every month we would have at least one or two training days. I used to enjoy them very much. On other occasions there would also be tactical training — how to deploy at different incidents and so on. Being an outdoor range, Otmoor was glorious on that sunny Wednesday morning. We spent the first few hours in straightforward firearms training.'

Sergeant Brightwell and his colleagues at the training range were the only officers from the Support Group on duty that day. The rest of the team were off duty, or just about to come on. Thus there was no tactical firearms cover in the south of the Thames Valley Police area at all. In policing terms, however, there is nothing remarkable about such a lack of cover, as the former policeman and firearms expert Colin Greenwood explains: 'Some people believe that you'll never be able to get a tactical unit into action quickly enough; that effective response times can only be achieved when weapons become available to many more local officers. When I was with the police we used to do tests. I would go back and pick a day — three o'clock in the morning on 4 August, say — and then demand of the Force how many armed men would have been available. And each time that was done, we were frightened by the result.'

The Government's reluctance to allow the police ready access to firearms can be traced back to the first half of the 1980s. For it was then that the police had made a series of disastrous mistakes with their weaponry. An innocent man, Stephen Waldorf, had been gunned down in his car in 1983, and then, two years later, Mrs Cherry Groce was crippled by police fire in Brixton. Only a few months later a five-year-old boy, John Shorthouse, was shot by a policeman in Birmingham. There was a huge public outcry and the seeds of a new approach were sown. Political pressures resulted in the Home Office issuing a directive that considerably more caution should be shown in the handling of firearms. As a result, the rank necessary to sanction an armed operation was increased from Inspector to the Assistant Chief Constable himself. The key to increased public safety, a Government working party later argued, was to have fewer firearms officers, more professionally trained.

Despite this new caution by the Home Office, by 1987 more than 14,000 British police officers were authorized to use guns. The prevailing legislation was then the Criminal Law Act of 1967. Sergeant Brightwell explains: 'We all used to have to carry a "white card" which showed our authority to use a firearm and which laid out the guidelines under which we could operate. The card quoted from the '67 Act, saying that "guns can be issued when there is reason to believe that a police officer may have to face a person who is armed or otherwise so dangerous that he could not safely be restrained without the use of firearms".'

The card also specified that guns should be fired by police 'only as a last resort when conventional methods have been tried and failed or must from the nature of the circumstances obtaining be unlikely to succeed if tried'. A gun could then be used, the legislation stated, when it 'is apparent that the police cannot achieve their lawful purpose of preventing loss or further loss of life by other means'. Sergeant

67

Brightwell and his colleagues in the Support Group were very familiar with the statute, for the extremely cautious wording of the 1967 Act had been drummed into them time and again.

But for all the Group's members, there was one crucial consideration which always put the entire issue into perspective: that while the decision to open fire is an individual one, that individual's decision might one day have to be justified before a properly constituted court of law. Sergeant David Warwick, a colleague of Brightwell's, was not actually in the Support Group. But as a firearms instructor who sometimes supplemented the Tactical Firearms Team's response, he was well acquainted with the regulations concerning firearms.

On the implications of this rule, Sergeant Brightwell says: 'Just to fire for the sake of it quite simply makes you a murderer. If I have a person within my sights — even if he has shot another person — I quickly run through three simple tests. Is the person likely to shoot anybody else? Is there any threat to the public, the police or anybody else? And is the person likely to abscond or commit other offences? If the answers to these questions are coming up no, then you simply do not shoot. In fact if you have to shoot we in the Support Group consider it basically a failure of policy. We are the police. We are not judge, jury and executioner all in one.'

Britain's police, both armed and unarmed, are therefore quite properly prohibited by Act of

Parliament from using unreasonable force. But at the same time it is accepted that the police should not be obliged to expose themselves to unnecessary risks while carrying out their duty to protect the public. While this is an extremely delicate balance to achieve, Chief Inspector Glyn Lambert is sure of one thing: 'When an armed incident occurs it is an impossibility to just go charging in like the Cavalry. Of course we have a duty to save lives if one can. But it is just not on to expose yourself to a ridiculous amount of jeopardy in order to do this. So if necessary we will go cautiously. And if necessary we might even have to go tortuously. I have to protect the public, of course. That is what policing is all about. But I am never going to be prepared to sacrifice my men like lambs to the slaughter needlessly and without a sense of direction or knowledge of what they are trying to achieve.'

There are many other facets to policing besides the firearms issue, which is why, when a major incident occurs, overall operational control immediately passes to the Assistant Chief Constable. And on Wednesday, 19 August 1987 this senior position was occupied by Charles Pollard, perhaps the most popular and highly respected person in the entire Thames Valley force. On that Wednesday morning Assistant Chief Constable Pollard was preoccupied with one thing: that his desk should be cleared by the end of the afternoon, for his long-awaited summer leave was due to begin.

One Bloody Afternoon

A veteran of the siege at the Iranian Embassy in London in 1980 and of the bombing of the Conservative Party conference in Brighton in 1985, Pollard has been a lifelong defender of the principle of Britain's police remaining unarmed: 'The Thames Valley Police is, in common with the rest of the police service in this country, a civil, unarmed police force whose members carry out their duties through the consent of the community rather than by force. On those occasions when force is required, tradition provides, and the law dictates, that only the very minimum of force is permissible. This principle is practised not only in everyday policing situations but it is also enshrined in all our policies involving the exercise of force through the use of special equipment such as firearms. What a lot of people don't realize is that when an incident occurs it's not just a question of going into a local police station, getting a gun, going out and shooting a suspect. It's just not as simple as that. It does take time to get weapons out, to get them to the scene, to identify where your suspect is and then to contain him. And that is one of those things which, in a country like ours, we perhaps have to accept.'

As the Assistant Chief Constable set about his paperwork, hoping to be able shortly to go on holiday with a clear conscience, Sergeant Brightwell was engaged in his training session at the army range at Otmoor. Then, suddenly, Brightwell's pager sounded. Almost simultaneously, Sergeant Warwick's did likewise. So did those belonging to the firearms instructors. For the last few minutes or so, Kidlington HQ had become frantic with activity. Chief Inspector Lambert, head of the Support Group, was swinging into action, his many years of experience in the police standing him in good stead in a crisis. The Assistant Chief Constable phoned home to break the news to his wife that their holiday was off. Although they did not know it at that time, the members of the Tactical Firearms Team of the Thames Valley Police were poised to confront the biggest ever test for armed police anywhere in the United Kingdom.

7.
'A Man in Black has shot my Mummy'

At home in North Newnton, Nellie Fisher waited and waited. It was a frustrating time for the great grandmother on her ninety-fifth birthday; she was growing impatient for the festivities to begin. So too were the other members of the family who had gathered for the occasion. But they all knew very well that the celebrations could not get under way until her favourite granddaughter, Little Sue, had arrived with young Hannah and James.

When Michael Ryan woke up that same morning he was feeling a little off colour. He decided that the best remedy would be to take a couple of paracetamols. Nor was he sure precisely how the day was likely to turn out. But one thing was certain: unlike the previous day, he would not be visiting the Tunnel Rifle and Pistol Club in Devizes, the shooting centre where he had been spending so much of his time and energy during recent weeks. Instead, having put on an open-necked white shirt and a pair of blue jeans, he jumped into his D-registration Vauxhall Astra and pulled out of his driveway in South View.

After turning right on to Fairview Road, Ryan then drove down Hungerford's ancient High Street and headed off towards the A4. He was travelling in a westerly direction, towards the Savernake Forest. It was that well-known Wiltshire beauty spot that 'Little Sue' had chosen for her picnic, with Hannah and James. She had prepared the children's treat some time before. Indeed she had meticulously planned out their activities for almost every day of those long summer holidays, which, for Hannah at least, still had another three weeks to run. And the weather, that Wednesday morning, had not let them down.

Myra Rose, a spirited pensioner of seventy-five, had also been in the forest that morning. Her home was in Bournemouth, but she was staying with friends in nearby Marlborough. The woodland setting was so soothing that she decided to sit down and read for a while, and before she knew it, almost an hour had slipped by. Her imagination and intellect exercised, she knew that it was time now for her body to benefit likewise. Walking along at a brisk pace, she basked in the glorious sunshine. Suddenly her serenity was shattered by a calm announcement from a little girl. It was four-year-old Hannah, Little Sue's eldest child.

'I was walking through the forest,' Myra Rose would later recall, 'when these two small children strolled up towards me. "Oh, we've been looking for you," the little girl said to me. "We were coming to find you!" They both held my hands and the little girl looked up at me and said: "A man in black has shot my mummy!" They were both very calm and didn't really seem at all dazed. "He's taken the car keys," said the little girl, "and James and me can't drive the car without the keys!" Then she said: "We've had our picnic — I'm going home to find my daddy. We're going home!" They then began to walk off. Well, this was a story you just could not believe. In any case, I hadn't heard any shots or anything. I was quite simply dumbfounded.'

Dumbfounded though she was, as a grandmother of two children Myra Rose knew full well that she could not allow these two youngsters to wander off all alone into the thick of the forest. Instinctively, without hesitation, she took them under her wing. For the first few moments, however, she was not sure what to believe, in which direction to head or indeed what to do at all. The little girl's story simply sounded too farfetched to be true. The kindly old lady, instantly adopted by Hannah and James, decided that she should perhaps go back in the direction the two children had come from and try to find their mother's car. She was convinced that somewhere in the forest was a young mother frantically searching for her two children.

Whether the little girl's story was true or not, Myra Rose knew that her role was to care for these two tiny waifs; to comfort and to calm them. As she embarked on her search, she knew that when it came to distracting or entertaining young children, one of her stories could almost always be relied upon. They had served her well with her own grandchildren in Australia, and, she hoped, they would have the same effect now.

'The children told me that they had been tired and had had a little sleep in the car,' Myra Rose would later explain. 'They then said that they didn't know the way back. So we walked back the way I had come from and we met some other people who I had earlier seen having a picnic. Then James began to cling to me. He just would not leave me. It was just such an incredible story, though, I was still not at all sure what to believe.'

Unfortunately, as the adoptive grandmother was shortly to discover, little Hannah could hardly have been a more reliable witness. Her every single word had been true. A man in black had indeed shot her mummy. And that man was Michael Ryan.

During their picnic, Hannah would later disclose to the police, another car was parked nearby, with a man sitting at the steering wheel. Just as her mother was finishing the picnic and folding away the groundsheet, the man had got out of his car and walked towards Little Sue and her children.

Ryan was brandishing a Beretta self-loading pistol, capable of firing sixteen shots. Pointing it at Little Sue, he told her to put her children into her own car. As she strapped them in, she succeeded in keeping her composure, speaking confidently and reassuringly to them. 'I'll be back in a few minutes,' she said.

Sue Godfrey's overriding priority was to give the impression that nothing out of the ordinary had happened, that she remained fully in control of everything that was taking place, just as she always did. In reality, as she knew only too well, something quite extraordinary had happened, and Ryan's Beretta amply demonstrated that she was not at all in control.

The gunman frogmarched Little Sue into a woodland glade some seventy-five yards from her car, clutching the blue tarpaulin groundsheet under his arm. There is little doubt that Ryan had sex uppermost in his mind when he approached Sue Godfrey, a strikingly attractive woman in her mid-thirties. Certainly the police have long taken this view. 'Of course, our theory is difficult to substantiate,' a police spokesman explains, 'because facts are scarce, and we only have the testimony of the little girl. But Mrs Godfrey was a very good-looking woman being led deep into the woods, with Ryan holding the groundsheet, to boot, so we don't think that he was taking her on a nature trail. We think that she must have tried to make a run for it. And that in so doing got shot.'

Hannah Godfrey heard those shots. She then saw the man in black run back to his car and speed off. Not surprisingly, there was no sign of her mother. Indeed, mother and children were never to set eyes on one another again. Hannah and James remained in the car for a short while before Hannah decided to unstrap herself and James.

What Hannah did not know was that her mother had been shot ten times in the back. After she had fallen through a wire fence, Ryan had then fired three more shots into her body. The pathologist Dr Roger Ainsworth later confirmed that he had found thirteen bullet holes in her upper back. But it was a policeman, Sergeant Coppen, who had been first to arrive at the scene of the crime. He found Sue's car parked on Grand Avenue in the forest, unlocked and with two handbags, several toys and her driving licence inside. He had found her body lying on its side at around 2pm on that warm Wednesday afternoon. Several bullet holes had punctured the blue, flowery dress which she had chosen to wear for Grandma Nellie's birthday. Ten yards away lay the blue groundsheet. It had been stretched out on the ground, but her clothing remained entirely undisturbed.

'A Man in Black has shot my Mummy'

Driving home from work that evening, Brian Godfrey heard on the radio that a young mother of two had been shot dead in the Savernake Forest. 'I thought, how terrible. Obviously I identified with a mother and two kids. But I never dreamed that it was my wife and kids,' Brian recalls.

When he returned to Burghfield Common, the family home in Clay Hill Road was empty. By the time another hour had elapsed the computer technician was distinctly on edge. Then he noticed two tall men walking down the path and making their way towards his front door.

'They were in plain clothes, but I knew that they were policemen. By the time they were inside I knew that Sue was either hurt or dead. One of them said, "You look upset," and I said that I had been listening to the car radio. Then they said: "We've got bad news for you — your wife is dead." I asked what had happened to the children and they told me that they were at Swindon police station. What I've managed to get from the children is that a man with a gun appeared just as they had finished the picnic. He apparently said to Sue: "I'm going to shoot you if you don't come with me." She fastened the children into their seats and told them that she would return in a short while.'

Sue Godfrey did not return — Ryan had seen to that — and her children were left to wander about the forest before being found by Myra Rose, who would later explain: 'I eventually went with the children to Swindon police station. Of course there were lots more stories throughout the day. James was with me all day until his daddy turned up. But when that poor man walked in, I thought that it was a good time for me to creep silently away so that James, in particular, would not notice that I'd gone.'

ITN's *News at Ten* broadcast to the nation later that evening the story of what had happened to Sue Godfrey and her two children, a story that was almost 'unbearably painful', even to report. As far as Ryan was concerned, however, the day had hardly begun. For as he sped away from the scene of this brutal murder, Mrs Kakoub Dean of the Golden Arrow Service Station on the A4 at Froxfield, was herself about to come within a hair's breadth of losing her life.

The isolated petrol station was the one where Sue Godfrey had filled up earlier that morning. She and Mrs Dean had exchanged a few brief but friendly words. A couple of hours had passed since then and Mrs Dean had served a good many more customers. For her, it was a typical August day at the Elf service station owned by her husband, Zubair, who also ran a petrol station at Marlborough. Then Ryan's silver grey Vauxhall Astra GTE pulled in. For several years now, he had been a regular customer and a familiar, if not always very friendly, face. Mrs Dean, a twenty-nine-year-old Asian mother of three, immediately thought it unusual that he had approached from the

Marlborough side, rather than from Hungerford, his customary route.

Almost every other day Ryan would buy £4 or £5 worth of petrol with his Barclaycard. He preferred pump number two, but this time, as well as putting £15.42 worth of petrol in his car, he filled a five-litre can with £2.01 worth.

'I also thought it a little odd that he had bought more petrol than usual,' Mrs Dean would later recall. 'I always used to say good morning to him, but he would never say a word. He would always just put his credit card down on the counter and never said anything. Not even a thank you. I must say that I always found him a very strange customer.'

Whatever lack of courtesy Ryan might have displayed in the past, Mrs Dean was certainly right about his behaviour being odd that day. For as she turned to the till to register the sale, he seemed to be bending down to remove something from the boot of his car. When she looked up again, Kakoub Dean was staring into the muzzle of a semi-automatic rifle: 'He seemed to be fiddling with the boot of his car for ages, waiting for another customer to leave. I can't remember whether I dived below the counter before the gun went off or after.'

Whatever the sequence of Kakoub Dean's movements, a one-inch hole had been blasted through the petrol station's window, the bullet ricocheting off the wall into the ceiling and out again into the back of the shop: 'The next thing I knew was a bullet had smashed through the glass kiosk screen and hit the clock. I don't know how it missed me, because I'm sure I felt it pass through my hair. It was just as I was telling him the amount on the till that I lifted my eyes and saw him pointing this gun straight at me.'

Ryan had missed. But he now stepped inside to do the job properly. Perhaps at closer range he would achieve a little more accuracy. Stunned, Kakoub Dean hid under the counter. 'Please don't, please don't,' she begged, as the gunman confronted her.

'I really don't know if he heard me or not. Because he said nothing. I could see him but he couldn't see me. He stayed there for a few seconds and was standing holding the gun — but there was nothing I could do.'

As she lay helpless under the counter, Kakoub Dean crawled close to a rack of sweets which formed part of its display. She held her breath and simply waited to die. There was nothing else she could do. She had appealed to Ryan, and it had had the air of a last request. As she did so, the gaunt face of Rambo looked out from the shelves, among an array of other violent and soft-porn videos, including *The Terminator*.

But all Kakoub Dean heard was the clicking of an empty gun: Ryan, the self-styled marksman extraordinaire, had run out of ammunition. 'I heard four or five clicks — and nothing happened,' she recounts. 'I know I am lucky to be alive. He would have killed me. I don't know how I survived. Because there was murder in his eyes. He didn't smile. He didn't blink. He didn't do anything. He just stared straight through me as if I wasn't there.'

Kakoub Dean had been spared. Little Sue had not. And not long after Ryan sped off from the petrol station, Detective Constable John Tuften, a scene of crime officer, arrived at the Savernake Forest to gather evidence with which he would later be able to compile a report or use in evidence. He took away a number of items, including bloodstained leaves, a fragment of wood, three cartridge cases and the blue groundsheet. The following day he returned and removed an additional ten cartridge cases and three bullets. The latter were embedded six inches in the ground.

The investigation into the murder of Sue Godfrey continued apace, and although it was not at all complicated, there were the customary procedures to be followed. Thomas Warlow, a forensic scientist based at the Home Office National Firearms Laboratory in Huntingdon, was soon able to confirm Detective Constable Tuften's earlier findings. He would later report to the inquest that he had observed two separate groups of spent 9mm cartridges on the ground. Thirteen pistol cartridges, of German manufacture, had indeed been fired. And there was not the slightest doubt in his mind that Ryan's Beretta had been responsible. For this pistol, which was in good working order, was later found attached to Ryan's right wrist with a bootlace, and covered with blood.

Nellie Fisher and her family continued to wait for Sue and the children. But by 1pm, as Ethel Fisher explains: 'We thought perhaps there had been an accident. We knew Sue would never just change her mind and return home without letting us know somehow. In the meantime, Joan's husband rang to tell Joan she wasn't to travel back home [to Reading] on her own, owing to a shooting at Hungerford. We then telephoned the police to hear what was going on, as Sue hadn't arrived. They informed us that she had probably been turned back, owing to the trouble. We then sat in Joan's car to listen to the radio and heard that a young woman had been shot dead at Savernake Forest, and that there were two children walking about — ages two-and-a-half and four-and-a-half. Knowing that she was stopping there to picnic with the children, we knew it was our Sue.

'The police were contacted again and certain questions were asked by them, and they said they would be coming round to see us. Which of course they did, and told us as gently as they could what had happened. Later we were taken to Swindon police station to collect the children. Brian, Sue's husband, was already there.'

By 12.40 that morning Michael Ryan had savagely murdered Susan Godfrey and bungled his attempt to kill Kakoub Dean. Immediately after his hasty exit from the service station, the shocked cashier telephoned the police — the first of what would soon become an avalanche of callers. But by this time Ryan was speeding back towards Hungerford.

Just as the serenity of Myra Rose had been destroyed earlier that day, so now the calm of that quiet market town was about to be shattered.

8 .
'A Funny Sort of Grin on his Face'

'That Wednesday afternoon I was driving around and about the Lambourn Downs, calling on customers on behalf of my employers,' recalls Ron Tarry, the then Mayor of Hungerford. 'Then the BBC announced on one of its early afternoon news bulletins that reports were coming in of a series of shootings in Hungerford. It said that someone had gone berserk in the High Street. I thought that this couldn't be our place. Not that I knew of another Hungerford, mind you. And then it said that it was Hungerford in Berkshire. So it had to be our town. My daughter was at our house with her friend and their children. I thought that they might well have gone down to the

High Street. I immediately decided to go back home to make sure that they were all right.'

As Ron Tarry drove home, the town was bustling with shoppers. For generations Wednesday had been market day and therefore the busiest day of the week. It is the one day of the week, Tutti Day apart, when the town really comes to life, with market stalls and shoppers all around.

Michael Ryan was also in town that day. He arrived there just before a quarter to one, fresh from his encounters with Sue Godfrey in the Savernake Forest and Kakoub Dean at Froxfield. He was poised to embark on an orgy of violence and slaughter that would, in just over one hour, leave sixteen people dead and as many injured. During the six years of the Second World War, twenty-eight men from Hungerford gave their lives for their country, heroes in the fight against fascism. But it was to take Michael Ryan a little over sixty minutes to reach almost two-thirds of that toll. He was about to turn a quiet Berkshire town into the most gruesome of killing fields. And in so doing, he was about to perpetrate the worst series of shootings in the history of British crime.

But the first thing Ryan did when he arrived back in Hungerford was to return home. He was seen going into 4 South View, and slamming the door behind him. According to a neighbour, Mrs Margery Jackson, he looked extremely uneasy: 'He looked at me in a very vague frame of mind as if he had been upset or angry and he went inside the house.'

Having committed one murder and bungled a second attempt, Ryan was well aware that it would not be long before the police would catch up with him. In this, at least, he was right. For two 999 calls had already been made, one at 12.40pm to the Thames Valley Police and the other at 12.42pm to the Wiltshire Police. This second call was from Kakoub Dean, urgently reporting that she had been shot at. Ryan's strategy now was to try to escape, to cover up as much of the evidence of his crimes as possible and somehow survive. After thoroughly dousing with petrol the home to which, twenty-seven years earlier, he had been brought back as a baby, he set it alight.

Ryan's survival kit and three firearms were in his car, and it was his intention to set off again from Hungerford. But as he was about to discover, things were not to go quite as planned. Not that there were any problems with his survival kit, for this he had thoroughly prepared. Safely tucked away in the boot of his car, it included a respirator mask, a flak jacket, battledress trousers and a balaclava helmet with eyeholes. The rucksack contained a first aid kit in a pouch, and there were also ear mufflers, a NATO poncho, a shoulder holster and a kitbag. In fact Ryan had been so meticulous in his preparations that among all the army surplus gear was a spare pair of clean blue and white underpants.

Nor was there anything wrong with his beloved firearms. As neighbours, strangers and passers-by alike were about to discover, these were all in good working order. The semi-automatic Kalashnikov — his latest acquisition and indisputably the pride and joy of his collection — in conjunction with the M1 carbine and the Beretta pistol, could not fail, he believed, to ensure his survival. These two rifles and one handgun were also in the car, having accompanied him to Savernake earlier that morning. But in reality Ryan's flight from Hungerford was never to get under way. It would have done 'if only my car had started', the gunman would later lament. The engine flatly refused to turn over.

It was perhaps no surprise that Ryan's car would not start. For almost a year he had driven it recklessly, travelling just under 18,000 miles and managing to wear all the tyres almost bald, when they should have lasted at least twice as long. That vehicle had been singularly abused from the start. Nonetheless, after his armoury, it had been the second and only other love of Ryan's life, and the source of innumerable squabbles with neighbours' children who threatened even to approach it or indeed its hallowed driveway. But now, spraying it with five bullets, he narrowly missed the petrol tank, although he succeeded in causing an explosion outside his home, already set ablaze by his own hand. However, turning his machine-gun on the car was one thing; turning it on his neighbours, quite another.

Almost immediately, round at the back of his house, Ryan took aim at his neighbours. Roland

Mason, a keen and able gardener, had been in his garden creosoting the fence of his home at 6 South View. He had planned to finish the fence while the children from number five were away on holiday. But he was never to complete the task, for he died instantly, after being shot six times. His wife, Sheila, then met the same fate, fatally wounded by a single shot which hit her in the head as she stood at the back of the house. The Hungerford massacre had begun.

Kitted out in an olive-green armoured waistcoat, and armed to the hilt with both weaponry and ammunition, Ryan would now dispense death and injury at whim. For those unfortunate enough to cross his path, destruction and death loomed. And in his choice of victims he would show no discrimination. A young punk rocker or a pensioner confined to a wheelchair: to Ryan neither age nor infirmity made the slightest difference — they were all legitimate targets.

Ryan next turned his guns on Margery Jackson, the neighbour who had noticed him arrive home a few minutes earlier. She had soon after seen Ryan emerging from his home and start firing at anything that moved, even a neighbour's dog. Diving for cover behind tables and armchairs, she had managed to telephone her husband, Ivor, to warn of the impending danger. Ivor insisted on coming straight back home, and his employer, George White, immediately offered him a lift. Then Ryan spotted her.

'I realized I'd been shot,' Mrs Jackson would later testify. 'There was a sort of burning pain in the back. In fact quite a few bullets came into my home. He was jogging up and down, running up and down the lane outside. He must have run up and down the lane about ten times. I think he was determined to slaughter us up there. It was all very quick fire.'

As Mrs Jackson lay injured in her home, she could hear gunfire continuing outside. But at least she had succeeded in her desperate struggle to pull a neighbour, seventy-seven-year-old Mrs Dorothy Smith, inside. Mrs Smith was one of the lucky ones that Wednesday, particularly since, although deaf in one ear, she had upbraided the gunman for disturbing neighbours with his gunshots, unaware that the shootings had signalled the start of the Hungerford killings.

Mrs Smith would later recall: 'I said: "Is that you making that noise? You are frightening everybody to death. Stop it!" He just turned his head to the right and looked at me. He had a terrible vacant look in his eyes and a funny sort of grin on his face. He looked to me as if he was brain-dead. I realized I was talking to Michael Ryan. I had, after all, known him for twenty years. But he looked so strange that day, I hardly recognized him. So I just yelled out to him that he was a stupid bugger.'

And she lived to tell the tale. Ryan then ran eastwards up South View and towards a footpath leading to Hungerford Common, shooting and injuring two people as he went. One of them was fourteen-year-old Lisa Mildenhall. Lisa was playing in the back of her home when she first heard the commotion outside. As Ryan stood near to her, she looked him straight in the face.

'I saw this man jogging along the road. He was carrying a great big rifle under his arm as if he was going to fire it. I stopped at the front door and the man stopped jogging as well. I immediately recognized him as Michael Ryan. I fixed my eyes at his eyes and he smiled at me. He then crouched down and aimed the rifle at me. I just froze by the front door. He fired the gun and I can't actually recall being hit. I thought he was playing about and that it wasn't a real gun, and that the blood was a blood capsule. I remember thinking, what a mess, and turned and ran inside. As I was running I could still hear shots being fired. I said: "Mummy, Mummy, have I been shot?" She looked really shocked and then I realized I had been. There was a lot of blood. I felt weak and fell to the floor.'

Lisa had been shot because, like many others in Hungerford that day, curiosity had got the better of her. Whereas her younger sister was able to take cover as Ryan approached, Lisa had stood there transfixed and was shot four times in the legs and stomach, the bullets splattering her pink leggings with blood. She might well have died had it not been for the timely actions of Mrs Sylvia Pascoe, a St John Ambulance Brigade worker, and another neighbour, Mrs Fiona

Pask, both of whom staunched her heavy bleeding while waiting for an ambulance. Unfortunately, as many of the dying and dead were to discover, ambulances were some time in coming, for the police had decided that it was too dangerous for the crews to make contact with the injured.

The road where Ryan had played as a small boy was now heavy with the smell of cordite. Its paths were bloodstained, and there was shattered glass and live ammunition scattered all around. As Ryan took the path towards Hungerford Common, local man Ken Clements was returning from a stroll with other members of his family. Unlike Ryan's first three victims, Ken Clements had received a warning that someone had 'gone berserk with a gun'. He had not believed a word of it, and had even gone out of his way to reassure another neighbour, Mrs Josephine Morley, that it was nothing more than children larking about. But Ken's son, Robert, was not quite so sure: 'I felt I couldn't let him go up there on his own, so I followed a few yards behind. Then this military-type person jumped out on to the track and lifted the gun and fired. My father seemed to fold up on to his back. I stared at the person holding the gun and I looked at the fence and I thought, right, I'm going to have to make a jump for it — and over I went. There didn't seem to be any way of helping.'

As Robert Clements clambered over the fence and into the adjoining school, he shouted out: 'He's shot the old man.' Ken Clements's sister and his two daughters did likewise, and ran, quite literally, for their lives. In fact Ken Clements died while trying to comfort his dog, which had been startled by all the shooting. When the pathologist examined the former soldier's body he was to find the dog's lead still clasped firmly in his hand.

A little later that afternoon Ron Tarry arrived back in Hungerford. He recalls: 'When I came into the town, I ran into a road block by the Bear Hotel at the corner, to come up the High Street. I saw someone I knew and asked what on earth was going on. This chap replied to me that a bloke had indeed gone berserk and that he had gone and shot someone at the end of my road. As you can imagine, this didn't really help a great deal because I still didn't know about my own family. As the Mayor of Hungerford, I was well aware of my responsibilities in relation to the community. But I must be honest and say that my first reaction was entirely personal. Were my family all right? What about my wife? What about my daughter Judith and her two small children, Stuart and David, who were there that day? I thought that since I knew all the back doubles I would get back to my home over the Common. But that was also blocked off. So instead I went to some friends of ours. No one knew what was going on, although by this stage there was a helicopter circling up above. The telephone system was completely overwhelmed. But I was lucky and managed to get through after just a few attempts. I spoke to my wife and daughter. Both told me that they were all right. Very selfishly, I was enormously relieved. Because I knew that all my other children were out of town. I then watched the television to try to find out what was going on.'

Liz Brereton, the wife of the Newbury-based traffic policeman PC Roger Brereton, did not have the television or radio on that Wednesday afternoon. She had returned to her home just outside Newbury, having completed her work as a home help. True, she had heard the sound of police sirens as she had gone on her rounds, but she had assumed that there had been a bad road accident and that she would hear about it from Roger later that evening. What she could not have known was that one of those sirens was her husband's. His patrol car was one of three ordered to keep a lookout on the A4 in response to what the police referred to on their radios as 'the Froxfield job', still unaware of the murder of Sue Godfrey in the Savernake Forest. None of these officers was armed. The first information reaching the officers in these early and preliminary reports was that no gun had been used. Within minutes, however, the message had been updated: 'Newbury have just had a call from a female in South View, Hungerford. We believe the bloke in connection with the Froxfield job is there with a weapon. Person in this area discharging a shotgun. One person injured at this stage. No further details. Over.'

As Liz Brereton later put it: 'If you're a policeman

and you hear about some maniac, you don't stop to think, I'm a traffic cop, it's nothing to do with me — you just go.' She was right. Her husband had done precisely that and sped off towards South View, as had his colleagues driving the two other marked police cars. Between them they hurriedly devised a strategy. The incident could best be contained, they thought, by blocking off both ends of South View. PC Brereton's car would go to the west entrance, nearest the town, while the other two would approach from the east, across the Common.

As he made his way to South View from the end allocated to him, PC Brereton realized the growing seriousness of the incident to which he had been called. The police radio network was now buzzing with reports of further 999 calls. Urgently, he radioed for an update: 'One-eight, copy. Is he still armed, over?'

'Bravo sierra five, we have no knowledge at present, over. We assume so,' came back the reply.

That assumption was right. By now the gunfire in South View was almost continuous, as Ryan set about shooting at anything and everything within sight, including his beloved labrador, Blackie. As PC Brereton pulled into South View, police headquarters at Kidlington was urging the very greatest of care: 'HQ to all mobiles. Please treat with caution. The last report is that this person is armed and has used a shotgun and a person is injured.'

For PC Brereton, that warning came too late. In

what was undoubtedly the most savage of all the Hungerford killings, Ryan raked the police car with two dozen bullets, from both the Kalashnikov rifle and the Beretta pistol. As they peppered the car, one hit the policeman's neck, fatally wounding him. In total he had been shot four times. Slumped over the passenger seat of the car, but still clutching his two-way radio, he managed to pass on one last message: 'Ten-nine, ten-nine, ten-nine. I've been shot.'

It was police code meaning that an officer was urgently needing assistance. What PC Brereton did not know was that he had been fatally injured.

Forensic experts would later reveal that the pistol bullets were mainly confined to the front section of the vehicle and the windscreen. But the firing had continued down the nearside of the vehicle to the rear of it, and shots had also gone through the back window. In normal circumstances the bodywork of a car can usually be relied on to afford good protection against a pistol. But certainly not from a weapon as formidable as the Kalashnikov. Furthermore, the ammunition Ryan used throughout the massacre had been carefully chosen. It was imported and of Hungarian military manufacture. This differs from ammunition used by Western armed forces in that the bullet core is a hard steel slug in a copper-coated jacket. Classified as armour-piercing, these bullets were far better able to penetrate through the body of the vehicle and its fittings. The unarmed police officer had simply not stood a chance. Afterwards, not even sparing a look for his victim, Ryan had just run off.

For ambulanceman Adrian Coggins, the nightmare of Hungerford appears unlikely ever to end: 'One sight will haunt me for ever. That poor policeman with a bullet in his back. He was just an ordinary copper doing his job. A man like me, with a wife and kids back home.'

Liz Brereton was still oblivious to the carnage being inflicted in Hungerford. Having tended to the needs of others, she was now free to set about her own domestic routine, as she recalls: 'I was just going to put the radio on, as I usually do, but I suddenly stopped myself. It was as if I wasn't meant to hear. I thought that as it was such a lovely day I might as well clean the bedroom windows.'

The windows of her police house soon looked spick and span, and Liz moved on to the next item on the agenda: the washing. With two teenage sons living at home, there was seldom any shortage of work waiting to be done.

Meanwhile, Ryan continued to make his way along South View, away from the Common. As he did so, Mrs Linda Chapman and her sixteen-year-old daughter, Alison, came under fire. Alison had heard shots coming from South View and had told her mother that she was concerned for the horses she kept there. Together they had decided to investigate. Driving towards South View, they too soon came face to face with Ryan. As the windscreen shattered, Linda Chapman felt a shot hit her neck. She nonetheless managed to drive down Park Street to the doctor's surgery in The Croft, where mother and daughter both received emergency treatment, Alison having also been shot in the leg.

Audrey Vaquez witnessed Ryan's technique. It was hardly sophisticated, as she would later reveal to the inquest. She had watched, terrified, from behind her net curtains as the gunman, bearing two rifles and one handgun, waited for a victim, any victim, to approach.

'He took one step into the road as the car came around the corner, lifted the gun and then fired it at the driver's window. I heard smashing glass and then the sound of a car crashing.'

Satisfied that his victim was dead, Ryan would then stroll casually away to seek more human targets.

'He appeared so calm and walked on as if nothing had happened,' Mrs Vaquez continued, 'almost as if it was like a fairground game. There was no emotion whatsoever.'

Ryan was firing left and right, reloading from a bag of cartridges on the chest of his sleeveless flak jacket. As the medical authorities realized the scale of the shootings, urgent appeals were made for voluntary nurses to report for duty. More and more police descended on Hungerford, summarily ordering people off the streets. Crowds piled into the Three Swans Hotel, where there was an unseemly dash for the bar. Before long, the busy market-day town had become a ghost town.

Jennifer Hibberd came within twelve feet of Ryan as he stood with a rifle in one hand, so she was able to observe him at close quarters: 'His face was sweaty, with red blotches. I could see he had a strange smirk on his face, half grinning.'

The gunman's strategy was to cripple first, then to shoot again to kill. The shots were multiple and came from two weapons. His victims were incapacitated by shots from the Beretta, after which the coup de grace would be delivered by the Kalashnikov.

Near the other end of South View, as his own home burned, Ryan was killing again. His sixth victim was Abdul Rahman Khan, an eighty-four-year-old retired restaurateur, whom he shot twice with the Kalashnikov. Mr Khan had been in the back garden of his home at 24 Fairview Road, peacefully mowing the lawn. His wife, Bessy, would later describe how she had heard a terrible noise after her husband had gone into the garden. She heard him calling to her and saw that he had been shot. But Abdul Rahman was never to recover from his wounds.

Immediately after shooting Mr Khan, Ryan turned his gun on Alan Lepetit, who was walking along Fairview Road towards South View. The coalman had become extremely concerned about the safety of his children and, like the Chapmans, had set off to investigate. Ryan shot him twice in the arm, and then again in the back as he fled from the scene. Alan Lepetit could hardly have been better known to

Michael Ryan because he was his immediate neighbour. It was he who had once helped Ryan put up his gun cabinet, as his wife Linda would later recall: 'He had wanted a hand carrying the Chubb steel case upstairs to his bedroom. Ryan always liked to be surrounded by an armoury of guns, even when he was asleep.'

Unlike Mr Khan, Alan Lepetit survived.

Ambulancewoman Mrs Linda Bright had been based in Hungerford for just three weeks when she found herself, with Mrs Hazel Haslett, the first ambulance crew to arrive on the scene. As they tried to enter South View to tend to the injured, they too came under fire. Although Ryan's bullet shattered the windscreen of their ambulance, it ricocheted off and they were able to make a quick getaway because they had reversed into South View, instead of driving forwards. But even after coming under fire, with Hazel Haslett having received arm and leg injuries from flying glass, they both continued to give Ryan's victims first aid, before going on to answer a second call for help and managing to rescue four people who had been shot.

'As we turned into South View,' Mrs Haslett would later recount, 'I screamed to Linda: "Get out of here", and we backed away. When I heard him fire I was petrified. We could see a man running away from him bleeding. We were trying to get to him when the gunman fired.'

As they set about their hasty retreat, they managed

to send a quick radio message: 'Under fire, under fire,' while they drove away from the killing zone. The ambulance crew sought safety just round the corner, where their priority was to warn other crews who, because of the volume of calls, were bound to be approaching. But because part of Hungerford is a communication black spot for the ambulance service, a problem already hampering the police operation, they were not sure whether or not their message had been received. So they headed off towards a nearby old people's home to make sure that their urgent message came across loud and clear. They had acted decisively and with courage and were later honoured for so doing. In many respects, though, Linda Bright and Hazel Haslett had been lucky that Wednesday, as they would be the first to admit.

Liz Brereton was not to have such good fortune: 'I was shaking a mat out in the back garden. Then, out of the corner of my eye, I saw an unmarked car pull up outside our house, with a policeman and woman. And I remember thinking, ooh, hello, who's he dragged home for tea now. But then I saw my best friend also getting out of the car. I took one look at their faces and I knew it was bad news. I thought it was my eldest son, who had gone up to Wembley to see a Madonna concert. I thought that he had perhaps been killed during a traffic accident. All this was flashing through my mind. I thought, well, where is Roger if something has happened to our son? Then I thought that he was perhaps too upset to face me.

One Bloody Afternoon

When they told me that it was Roger, I said: "Don't you mean Shaun" — my son — because I was so convinced it was him. I had no idea what had been going on that day. As they talked about a terrible accident, I asked them outright: "Are you telling me that my husband has been shot?"'

Indeed they were.

'I knew that Roger had been killed,' Liz would later explain. 'And people were coming round all the time to comfort me. But I would end up by comforting them. They would come into the house and just burst into tears. They were crying but I couldn't. So I would just say, "It's all right", and comfort them. All I experienced was a lump in my stomach. When I did cry, there was nothing much. It was as if it just didn't seem to want to come. Then I had a couple of good ones, but I knew it wasn't all. At the beginning I almost felt sorry for that guy, almost. Because I thought for anyone to do that, they have to be completely sick in the head. But that didn't last long. I have been able to harness feelings of hate towards him, even though in so doing I know that I only hurt myself. But he robbed me of a future, and I'm angry about that. I know it sounds horrible to say so, but the truth is that I curse the day his mother gave birth to him. Because if it wasn't for him I would be a happy, contented woman. We had all sorts of exciting plans together for the future. It's often said that life begins at forty — so bang goes that bloody theory.'

When, seven weeks later, the Archbishop of

Canterbury addressed a memorial service in Hungerford, not surprisingly his words were a good deal more measured:

'What happened here in Hungerford on 19 August shocked this whole land. A small country town, long in history, rich in memories, beautiful in its surroundings. Surely this is the very epitome of the England of which poets have written and expatriates have dreamed. That such a place should, on a summer afternoon, erupt in gunfire and terror, blood and death, was, quite literally, shocking to us all.'

Just as the ambulance crews were prohibited from tending to Ryan's victims, so the fire crews were obliged to stand idly by for almost four hours as the terraced houses in South View burnt almost to the ground. It was, quite understandably, the constant risk of being shot at which prevented them from going in, as Divisional Officer John Cart explains: 'We tried to get crews in at about half-past one, but because of the amount of shots being fired we had to withdraw. The fire is believed to have started about 1pm. But it wasn't until 5pm that crews were permitted to enter. When we did go in, all four properties were quite badly damaged and involved in fire. What we did was to put a sprayjet at the end of the terrace to stop any fire spreading to the bungalow at the end. No personal effects were rescued from any of the houses. All that was left was four walls.'

After venturing briefly into Fairview Road, Ryan,

who had now fatally wounded six people, returned to South View. By this time Mr Ivor Jackson, who had earlier received a telephone call from his wife warning him of the catastrophe which was unfolding, was also making his way back into South View, along with his colleague George White, a quantity surveyor. Mr White was at the wheel of the car, having volunteered to drive Ivor home after Margery Jackson's call. Immediately, his Toyota came under fire, an arc of eleven bullets hitting the car. As George White died at the wheel, the car crashed into PC Roger Brereton's white patrol car. Ivor Jackson, also shot and injured, immediately realized that one wrong move and Ryan would move in to finish him off, as he would later explain: 'I saw that this police car ahead of us had hit a telegraph pole. The policeman was slumped inside. Suddenly our car was raked with machine-gun fire, with these bullets starting to come at us. I got three in the chest and I've still got one left in my head, which apparently went in through my ear. I realized that I had been shot and so I decided to play dead. But I still thought that I was going to die. Then, with Mr White no longer in control of his Toyota, we crashed into the police car ourselves.'

As Ivor Jackson feigned death, he hoped and prayed that Ryan would not come any closer in order to inspect his victims. His good fortune, however, was to be Dorothy Ryan's misfortune, for as he lay motionless in the passenger seat of the car, the gunman's mother was returning in her car from the local shops. Dorothy Ryan had been in excellent spirits of late, for she was looking forward to starting, in a few weeks' time, a new job at a stylish health farm just outside Hungerford. She parked her car behind George White's and emerged into a scene straight from a horror film. What she was about to confront was all the more horrific in that it was her only child, Michael, on whom she had doted for over a quarter of a century, who was the marauding murderer of South View.

Ivor Jackson recalls: 'I then heard somebody open the door of the Toyota and Ryan's mum looked in and said, "Oh, Ivor. . ." and she then went hurrying along up the road.' Another witness, Chris Bowsher, recalls seeing Dorothy Ryan at the bottom end of South View, talking to a man who insisted that she should not go home. But she was adamant that she should, and pushed her way past him, aware that it was her responsibility to reason with her son. As she ran towards the home that they shared, which was even now being consumed by flames, she threw up her hands in horror. 'Stop, Michael. Why are you doing this?' she shouted.

In reply, Ryan raised his gun. Understanding at once the danger she was herself now facing, Dorothy Ryan hastily changed her tone. No more remonstrations now; just an urgent plea for her own life to be spared. Amanda Grace overheard it: 'I heard a woman scream, "Don't shoot me", and then I heard two rapid bangs.'

As his mother slumped to the ground, Ryan shot her twice more in the back, from a distance of less than four inches. She had been shot with the Kalashnikov. Joining Ryan's toll of victims, now she too lay sprawled downwards in the road just in front of George White's car. Ivor Jackson, still pretending to be dead, heard it all.

Dorothy Ryan was the eighth person to die since the first murder back in the Savernake Forest. In all, six had been killed with the Kalashnikov, two with the Beretta. In fact, seven of Ryan's victims, his own mother included, had died in the small area of South View itself. As the terrified people of Hungerford locked themselves in their houses and cowered for cover, and as a police helicopter circling overhead warned by loudspeaker those living in the cordoned-off area: 'If you value your lives, stay indoors', there were now just two questions on everybody's mind. How long would Ryan be allowed to continue his slaughter without being challenged? And, more pertinently perhaps, where on earth were the armed police?

It was a question to which Roy Tarry, for one, certainly wanted an answer: 'I still didn't know what to believe. I kept saying to myself that this can't be true. Chicago, yes. Liverpool or the East End of London, perhaps. But Hungerford? Surely not. Many people felt awful for a very long time that afternoon because they just were not able to find out what was going on. All the time we were trying to get information. My daughter knew very well that she had to keep the children indoors and the windows closed. But it was a very hot day, so she spent the afternoon bathing the children twice. Round at my friends' house, we had tea, watched the television and talked. It wasn't until 7pm, when I managed to find a way back into Hungerford, through a back way, that I began to find out what had been going on. The name of Michael Ryan meant nothing to me, although subsequently I remembered seeing him. But no one, it seems, really knew him. My wife knew Dorothy quite well, though — a very pleasant woman. Many people saw bloodshed. I didn't, because the bodies had been removed by the time I reached the scene. But I did see some of the cars, bloodstained and with bullet holes, smashed windscreens, and so on. We are a very small community and it of course affects us all. We were all in state of shock. I thought, what on earth can people do? What can I do? What can be done? I didn't know what to do — just that something should be done. That we couldn't simply sit around.'

A little later that evening ITN made contact with Ron Tarry, as did the BBC. He immediately agreed to their requests. Unbeknown to him, however, the Mayor was about to have a role thrust on him. For he was to become, both nationally and internationally, the 'voice of Hungerford', instantly recognizable by his gentle Berkshire burr.

At the Tunnel Club in Devizes, where Ryan had

spent so much of his time during the previous few weeks, signing in virtually every other day in order to sharpen his shot, there was similar shock and outrage. 'Michael Ryan didn't give the slightest indication that he was a head case,' one of its directors would later insist. 'With hindsight, though, you can see that he was like a silent tiger.'

But the tiger had still only exacted half of his toll. Indeed for several hours on that black afternoon that same silent tiger had still to be located, let alone silenced. He was free to roam the lanes and alleyways of Hungerford, and thus to resume the killings anywhere, any time and entirely at his whim.

Ryan now slipped out of South View, heading across the adjoining playing field. No one saw him go.

9.
'Be Still, and know that I am God'

During the early part of the evening of Tuesday, 18 August, some sixteen hours before Michael Ryan embarked on his bloody rampage, the Reverend David Salt, Hungerford's vicar, was wrestling with an age-old dilemma. So too were other members of the Stewardship Committee of St Lawrence's church. While representatives were keen to promote the concept of Christian stewardship, they were equally adamant that any events they might organize should not be, or be seen to be, merely another round of fund-raising activities. The Committee members concluded that the only satisfactory answer was to actually demonstrate their love and care for the community of Hungerford. But how, in practical terms, was this to be done?

'The next day, Wednesday, 19 August, we had a kind of answer,' the Reverend Salt would later reflect. 'It was not the one we were looking for, of course. But soon there was to be no room for Christian theories of compassion and what we might do, for the task was all too plain.'

Shortly after lunch on that Wednesday afternoon the vicar was preparing for his weekly hospital visit. But before setting off, he had to make a number of important phone calls. However, each time he dialled a number the line was engaged. He thought that for so many numbers to be so consistently busy was a little strange, and concluded that there was probably a fault on the line. Leaving the vicarage in his gold-coloured Mitsubishi Colt, he set off towards Hungerford High Street. This time it was ambulances, not antiques, which caught his eye. For he soon found himself staring at an entire fleet of hospital vehicles, all from adjoining Wiltshire.

'They all looked clean and shiny. So I thought that maybe Wiltshire County Council had taken on a number of new ambulances and they were having a joy ride, or something like that.'

The Reverend Salt, a small, bespectacled man, had come to Hungerford three years earlier, having previously been based at Checkendon. In fact both Hungerford and Checkendon are Anglican churches falling within the Diocese of Oxford. But the

Reverend Salt's was the only Anglican church in Hungerford, and thus he was the community's only full-time Anglican minister.

'I was very happy to go to Hungerford,' the vicar would later recall. 'Before I took up my appointment I was invited to go along to see the church of St Lawrence and meet members of the community. I noticed straight away that many pews had been removed from the back of the church. This told me that they were a community church, and I liked that.'

The new vicar instinctively felt that the church, while active, was lacking in young people. There was an imbalance in the composition of the congregation, which he felt had to be redressed. And before long there was indeed movement in the air. One particularly committed parishioner, Mary Grayson, started a boys' choir almost from scratch. It was very successful, soon gaining a number of diocesan awards. The Reverend Salt also began to liaise with the schools in Hungerford and from the start found a warm welcome.

'I was very pleased with how things were coming along. I then got the girls to come in and do the serving at the altar in communion. Attendance began to creep up, and we eventually had three teams of six servers. And then we got a tiny tots' club going during the week.'

The Reverend Salt had been based at Checkendon for well over a decade when he first felt that the time was right for a change. But it was while working as chaplain at Borocourt Hospital, within the parish of Checkendon, that he had had his first contact with handicapped children, some of whom were triply afflicted, being deaf, dumb and mentally handicapped. As he explains, 'So you might say that I had some idea of tragedy already. Whatever you are faced with, you don't necessarily panic. Because you know that this is part of life.'

Unlike the majority of English clergy, the Reverend Salt also brought with him to Hungerford a wealth of experience from his time overseas. Having been based in the Pacific islands for eight years, he had served as a missionary in what is now the Church Province of Melanesia. Initially based on the island of Aoba, he had then moved to Pentecost Island, where two of his three children were born. From there it was to the Solomon Islands. It was an environment in which he had thrived, although there had been many moments when the vicar, his wife and their young children had found themselves truly alone.

'You would face cyclones and human tragedies with monotonous regularity,' the vicar recalls. 'Once a boat caught fire. People were badly burned. And, in the tropics, that hurts, believe you me. That time we were given medical help, but often we were just not able to get any medical assistance at all. So all of this was background training if you like. Even within our own family there was often malaria and high fever. Again, we simply had to sort it out ourselves. So too with the rough seas. Death was very much a reality.'

The Reverend Salt's curriculum vitae might reveal a distinctly international flavour, but his roots were solidly English. He was born and brought up in Berkshire, in a family who were all closely associated with the Church. Both David Salt and his brother had themselves sung in the church choir, and his older sister went on to become a parish worker and a missionary for twenty-two years. He was only thirteen when he began to feel some sort of calling to the ministry, a feeling which matured as his academic career progressed. With national service out of the way — three years in the RAF — he went on to graduate from King's College, London, with a degree in theology. From there it was straight out to the exotic islands of the Pacific; with him went his wife, who had sung in the very same church choir of his childhood.

As the vicar drew up in Hungerford that Wednesday afternoon, there was a knocking on the window of his car. It was a journalist from the *Daily Express* who, having spotted his dog-collar, was eager to obtain the minister's reaction to the carnage and slaughter unfolding by the moment in the town. But since the minister was unaware of what had happened, naturally he had nothing to say. Their roles reversed, the journalist rattled out what information he had so far been able to gather.

'When I arrived in the High Street I realized that something had happened,' the vicar explains, 'because there were still more ambulances this time from Berkshire. I then met Neal Marney, an ambulanceman I knew, and he told me that the best thing to do was to go home and lock your doors, because nobody knew where this man was, and that the gunman was still on the loose.'

It was sound advice. Heading back towards his home with the car radio on, the Reverend Salt, like the rest of the town, was desperate for information. But hard news was a scarce commodity in Hungerford that afternoon. Back in the vicarage, having wisely locked himself in, he continued to monitor the news bulletins, listening to the radio and television simultaneously. Some facts did begin to emerge, but much of the information was wildly inaccurate. Because whatever atrocities the gunman might have committed, the vicar already knew that they had not taken place in the High Street. That much he had seen for himself. That was just as well, because the High Street had been packed with market-day shoppers.

At 4pm the Reverend Salt's son, Stephen, having heard on the radio what had happened, managed to get through to his father on the telephone. He had been extremely concerned about the safety of both of his parents. Yet the vicar felt that his place should be in the town, where, whatever else was happening, there was clearly great suffering. So he set off again towards the town centre. Perhaps, on the streets, he would be able to find out just what was going on. He was soon to discover, however, that it was simply not possible to get through, for the whole of Hungerford had been sealed off.

Undeterred, ninety minutes later the vicar left the vicarage once again. He explains: 'By this time people were coming home from work. It was almost as though we were waiting in the High Street for carnival day. I remember that this struck me most forcibly, because by this stage all the people were lining the streets. But it wasn't a carnival. Many people were terribly worried, not knowing what had happened to their relatives. This was one of the worst aspects of the tragedy, the husbands coming back from work and not knowing about their families. Shopkeepers were coming out bringing people cups of tea. It reminded me so much of the last war: newsflashes coming through, people coming out to their gates and talking. People wanting to share the news.'

Not until 10 o'clock that evening would the determined vicar succeed in getting through to the area of the town which had been affected. Many doctors had likewise been prohibited from entering the killing zone. By now the name of Michael Ryan was on everybody's lips. And not just in Hungerford, but across the whole country. Yet Ryan was a stranger to St Lawrence's, and the vicar could only recall nodding to him in the street. In fact, as the

Reverend Salt was shortly to discover, Ryan was a stranger to everyone.

The vicar describes his reaction to what he discovered: 'I was just blank. All the time just trying to listen to people. At the same time a thousand things were going through my head. I felt numb, but also wanted to survey all the problems and keep an open mind — that is, not go round in circles, or panic. I also felt that though one was quite inadequate, as a vicar people expected you to act, and had faith in you to do the right thing — whatever your qualifications! I also remember thinking at the time that you go to church every morning to say your prayers. That you just keep this prayer machine ticking, so that it makes you ready to deal with a disaster when it happens. This gives you a sort of background of spiritual support. The vicar's role is finely balanced: you have to develop a hard skin whilst at the same time keeping a soft centre. If you are ever in a hard situation — what I do is to make what I call an arrow prayer — as though you are shooting a quick prayer up to God. This would be in terms of, say, the Psalms. You must get that phrase: "Be still, and know that I am God." That's a good arrow prayer from the Psalms. It is important to remember that God has looked on this situation maybe a million times before. In order to help people you have to be empty, so as to be receptive to what people are saying. Only then can you really think out the problem and try to give whatever help you can. Tragedies do happen all over the world. I know that this is a bad part of life's diet, but I have to say that it didn't come as a great shock to me. That's why, I think, I wasn't overwhelmed. I felt that there was the work waiting to be done and that now you just go and get on with it.'

Part of getting on with it, the vicar decided, was to take a measure of responsibility in dealing with the press. Once again, the able minister had had some experience in this role. Not that he had welcomed it at the time. For at Checkendon a person associated with the church had been accused of being a paedophile, and it was not long before the salacious Sunday press, most notably the *News of the World*, was beating hard at the cleric's door, eager for a reaction.

It was fortunate, too, that Ron Tarry and the Reverend Salt were already well known to one another, the mayor being a regular churchgoer. Mayor and vicar agreed that if they could deflect the media from hounding the bereaved, if only to a certain extent, that was a role which they could usefully perform. It was to be an allocation of labour which was to serve the town extremely well. The vicar also concluded that his priority was a pastoral one, visiting the injured and bereaved: 'The most important thing I could do was just be there. Maybe just to hold a hand, or to give a hug.'

What the Reverend Salt was not used to, however, was the notion of murder. Never before had he buried the victims of murder, or counselled those thus bereaved. He was also to be obliged to remind himself repeatedly that each bereaved or injured person was an individual, not a statistic. He knew full well that there would be little point in reminding people that they were not alone.

Quite apart from the work which was about to come his way in the aftermath of the tragedy, the vicar also had to perform his usual duties. Part of this work included ministering to those who had lost loved ones through natural causes. Therefore he also had to remind himself that their loss was as real and personal to them as that of those whose loved ones had been gunned down by Michael Ryan.

It was no surprise, then, that the Reverend Salt got little sleep in the weeks and months that followed the massacre. Yet he did not seem to need it; it was as if he was being carried through by a tidal wave of love and prayer. Nor was there a great deal of time to prepare sermons, even though they were clearly going to be monitored closely by the national press, quite apart from by his superiors. Yet sermons flowed from him with the greatest of ease.

'I wanted to sleep,' the vicar explains, 'but there seemed so much information in my head that had to be sorted out, and jobs to be done for the following day. It was as well that I had kept my spiritual dynamo ticking over. Because when a great surge of power was needed it seemed to be there. And God's strength was sufficient for me. The congregation of

'Be Still, and know that I am God'

St Lawrence's was really magnificent, and I quite simply could not have coped without their support. They didn't have to be asked — they just got on with it. I now realize that we are, all of us, constantly "in training" as Christians. But I never dreamed that I would myself end up in the front line.'

10.
'Hungerford must be a bit of a Mess'

As soon as his pager had sounded, Sergeant Paul Brightwell knew that it was his duty to make immediate contact with Thames Valley Police HQ at Kidlington. So too did other members of the Support Group, who, like Brightwell, had been training at the army firing range at Otmoor. The message was simple enough: the Tactical Firearms Team was now required in Hungerford. But no member of that élite group had any idea of the scale of the slaughter which was being inflicted on the people of that town and which the specialist police unit was now about to witness at the very closest of quarters.

'All we heard to begin with was that there had

been "a shooting incident in Hungerford",' Sergeant Brightwell recalls. 'Details were scant, so no particular adrenalin was going — well, no more than usual, that is. You have to remember that a lot of the incidents that we hear about turn out to be false alarms. I immediately set off with two or three other members of my party in one of our unmarked cars, a blue Vauxhall Cavalier, one equipped with a blue light and two-tone horns. On the way down there, lots was going on on the radio. I didn't want to interrupt, so I was just listening. I then began to get a bit keyed up because we heard that there was someone on the loose shooting people and that at least three people had been killed. And also that a PC had been shot. Then I realized the type of incident I might be going to. All we were lacking was weapons. We had our overalls and body armour with us. The firearms instructors, with whom we had been training, took the weapons, and we were all heading for the same rendezvous point. This was changed, en route, from Newbury to Hungerford police station. But this was still quite some distance to travel.'

It was a Newbury-based policeman, PC Jeremy Wood, who had been the first to radio to activate the system for calling out the armed police. He was normally PC Roger Brereton's partner, but on this occasion his colleague had left a little before him in a separate car. PC Wood's car had been the second police car to arrive on Hungerford Common, the officers from the first having taken cover after coming

under fire from Ryan. He recalls that he came
perilously close to losing his own life: 'He was firing
numerous rounds from the hip at us — and we could
hear the bullets passing by.'

Like Roger Brereton, PC Wood was a father of
two in his late thirties. It was he, having seen the body
of Ken Clements lying in an alleyway, who sounded
the alarm and informed his superiors that a major
shooting incident was taking place. Together with
Robert Clements, whose father had been shot, PC
Wood withdrew to a copse across the Common, the
nearest safe location. Immediately he set about
clearing the area of the many families picnicking
there, who, until that moment, had been enjoying the
summer sunshine. He then set up a temporary HQ on
the Common for the back-up he had requested,
established a roadblock and, most crucial of all,
continued to call for the police sharpshooters. It was
there too that Wood had heard on his radio PC
Brereton's desperate last message: 'Ten-nine, ten-nine,
ten-nine. I've been shot,' a few moments before he
died.

However, the assistance requested by PC Wood
was to be some time in arriving. For while the order
to send the Tactical Firearms Team to Hungerford was
given at eight minutes past one, it would be another
one hour and twelve minutes before the whole team
had arrived and was ready to go into action.

But Chief Inspector Glyn Lambert's specialist
squad, then speeding towards Hungerford, was only

one part of a two-tiered arms strategy employed by the Thames Valley Police. In fact, for a whole hour, as the Tactical Firearms Team was preparing to confront its biggest-ever challenge, the first-tier response had already been successfully activated. This had involved bringing in officers able to draw weapons from local armouries. In such circumstances their brief is invariably the same: to contain the situation until the arrival of the more specialized teams, which are more highly trained and have the know-how to confront a gunman on the loose.

By 1.18pm the first locally armed officer had arrived in the town. However, he simply went to PC Wood's rendezvous point on the Common and stayed there, waiting for the helicopter to arrive. A member of the Diplomatic Protection squad, he was more used to looking after VIPs. All the time, though, the chance to contain Ryan was slipping away. At 1.20pm the police had their last sighting of Ryan.

At 1.28pm a second locally armed officer arrived. He too was from the Diplomatic Protection squad and these officers would in turn be joined by four more from that unit before the arrival of the Tactical Firearms Team. It was fortunate that they had been training only some twenty minutes away, and had thus been able to mobilize rapidly. They did show more than a little hesitation, however, in moving forward in an attempt to find their man. In any event, as members of the Diplomatic Protection squad assembled around the Common, Ryan was all the time moving away from the police, across the playing field. In fact the police were not to see Ryan for another four hours. But this did not mean that the gunman had suddenly become inactive. On the contrary, seeking out another victim, he soon spotted seventy-year-old Betty Tolladay in her back garden.

'I heard this banging,' she recalls. 'I thought it was children with fireworks or something. A bit early, I know, but they do find all manner of things that make noises. So I went into the garden and said, "For God's sake, stop that noise — it's getting me down."'

Unlike Dorothy Smith, who had earlier called Ryan a 'stupid bugger' without drawing the gunman's fire, Betty Tolladay was immediately shot. The bullet entered her groin, exiting via her back and smashing the top of her hip, part of the pelvis and the sciatic nerve en route. At the back of her home in Clarks Gardens, she realized straight away that she was now battling for her life: 'I immediately fell to the ground. One leg was absolutely useless. But I sat up and dragged myself to my back door, got over the step somehow, don't ask me how, and along to the hall, and got the telephone off the table and dialled 999. I've only two words to describe what happened: pure agony.'

The emergency services were by now well aware of the scale of the disaster, if not yet of the plight of Betty Tolladay. During the twenty-four hours around the period of the shootings, the Newbury telephone exchange was to handle almost a quarter of a million more calls than its usual daily total, which inevitably hampered both police and ambulance personnel in their work. So when a kindly voice from the ambulance services assured the severely injured Betty Tolladay that 'Somebody will be along with you soon,' it was no doubt promised in good faith. But 'soon' was to be almost five hours later. The speed and scale of the slaughter had brought with it confusion and chaos.

As Betty Tolladay began her long wait for medical help, Ryan was continuing to claim more victims. Francis Butler, a twenty-six-year-old accounts clerk, was out walking his dog on a path in Hungerford's Memorial Gardens. Hit three times by Ryan's Kalashnikov, he sustained injuries to his groin and leg. Letting go of the lead, the young man turned and appeared to slip, holding his leg as he fell. The bullet travelled up through his body, leaving a gaping wound in his back.

Leslie Bean, deputy officer of the Chestnut Walk old people's home in Hungerford, was the first person to reach him. He found Mr Butler's body on its back and immediately noticed a rifle lying on the ground about fifteen feet away. Working feverishly to stem the flow of blood from the large exit wound, Leslie Bean knew that if he abandoned his impromptu first aid, death would not be long in coming. But then, with Ryan just around the corner, someone shouted out a warning to Mr Bean that if he did not himself now move he might well end up in a similar predicament.

That person had not minced his words, bellowing: 'Get your arse out of here. He is coming back.'

Only then had Leslie Bean fled to safety. By the time the ambulancemen got to Francis Butler he was dead.

This shooting was witnessed by a thirteen-year-old Hungerford schoolboy, Dean Lavisher, from the top of a slide in the recreation ground. Although the boy was himself recovering from a leg operation, he hobbled to a nearby telephone box to call for an ambulance. As he did so, Ryan fired at Andrew Cadle, who had been playing in the recreation ground with Dean. Andrew was not the only one in Hungerford on that Wednesday afternoon to have reason to be grateful for Ryan's inconsistent marksmanship, for as the gunman fired, the boy pedalled away on his bicycle, mercifully hearing the bullet strike a brick pillar instead of his own young frame. After shooting Francis Butler, his ninth victim, Ryan abandoned his M1 carbine in the Memorial Gardens. This did not mean, however, that he was now only lightly armed, for he still had both the Kalashnikov and the Beretta.

'As soon as we arrived in Hungerford,' Sergeant Paul Brightwell would later explain, 'I saw that other parties of the Support Group were there, as well as our equipment. We got kitted up immediately — all on the double — with weapons being issued at the same time. While we were doing this, I was telling members of my group to take various weapons and at the same time trying to pay attention to detail. Chief Inspector Glyn Lambert, as he then was, was in charge of the Support Group, and he had two inspectors under him. I didn't see him in Hungerford immediately. While there is a rank structure, it always tends to be looser on such occasions and it was the obvious thing to do to get kitted up. You have to act on your own initiative, although I wasn't sure precisely where I was to be deployed.'

The truth was that Sergeant Brightwell's boss, Chief Inspector Lambert, had no particular strategy firmly fixed in his mind when he had set off from the Kidlington HQ. He was desperate for just one thing: hard facts. But amid the hysteria and chaos, reliable information was to prove very elusive. Because the local communications network had been completely overwhelmed by the volume of calls, many of the reported sightings of Ryan were wildly inaccurate, completely confused or just simply out of date. By the time the Chief Inspector arrived, however, he concluded that only three of the purported numerous sightings of Ryan could possibly have any credibility and were therefore to be pursued. One was on Hungerford Common, the other in South View and the third alleged sighting at the John O'Gaunt School. All three would have to be investigated and Chief Inspector Lambert divided up his troops accordingly.

'When we arrived in Hungerford,' the head of the Support Group would later comment, 'we of course had to locate and isolate Michael Ryan. But on the way down, apart from learning about the scale of the killings, I also heard that he had a high-powered rifle a hell of a lot more powerful than the shotguns I knew were ahead of us. So I knew straight away that containing Ryan was going to be an extremely difficult task, and all the more so because he was moving about. We put on our ballistic helmets, flak jackets and so on. We couldn't do this inside Hungerford police station, because there simply wasn't enough room to get in there. So we did it outside on the street instead. And since we didn't know if he would appear while we were briefing, some of our officers covered us while we were kitting up and everyone was being allocated their specific roles by me. Of course I would like to think that the approach was professional — but one very real difficulty was the confusion of all the reported sightings, not to mention all the people crying and sheltering at the police station. I wanted to get an armoured vehicle, to help us move freely around the streets, and I also wanted to get the helicopter into action as soon as possible, since it is an excellent spotting tool in which I have the very greatest of faith.'

At Hungerford's swimming pool Carol Hall, an air stewardess who lived locally, sensed that there was danger in the air. She had been talking to her grandmother, who ran a shop at the swimming pool, when she heard several rapid bursts of gunfire. Fearing that the person firing was approaching the pool, she immediately liaised with Michael Palmer, the pool supervisor and David Sparrow, a lifeguard. As the young lifeguard went outside, he saw the body of Francis Butler lying in the Memorial Gardens, with Ryan standing nearby. They immediately called all the swimmers out of the pool, evacuating some twenty children and several adults to the relative safety of the changing rooms. In due course the three would be commended for their bravery.

As they did so, Marcus Barnard, one of Hungerford's most popular personalities, was driving in his Peugeot towards Bulpit Lane to pick up a fare. He was known to almost the entire town as Barney the Cabby, and was one of just two drivers serving the community. He had been running his own business for just a few years and, together with his wife Jenny, was still celebrating the birth of his first child, Joe. The boy had not come to the Barnards easily, having taken the best part of six years to arrive. But when, finally, little Joe came into the world, he had done so prematurely. During his wife's pregnancy Barney had made no secret of the fact that he was hoping for a little girl, but when his son made his early appearance in the world, he was as thrilled as could be, as Jenny Barnard explains: 'Barney was so proud of the baby. Before he was born I used to pull his leg about changing dirty nappies and so on. He used to say: "You won't catch me changing a dirty nappy!" But he did absolutely everything for that baby. Bathed with him, played with him. He was just so proud.'

'Hungerford must be a bit of a Mess'

As he made his way along Bulpit Lane the thirty-year-old cabby appeared to notice Ryan, by then leaving the Memorial Gardens, and slowed down. Seconds later he was dead, a shot from Ryan's Kalashnikov having pierced the windscreen and caused a massive injury to the top of his head. Ryan had seen to it that Marcus Barnard was to be a father to baby Joe for just five weeks.

Kenneth Hall, a local government officer, witnessed the taxi-driver's savage and summary execution: 'I could not believe what I had just seen. I stopped in my tracks. The man threw the gun to the floor in front of him as if in disgust. He looked down at the gun and shook his head from time to time. He looked bewildered as if he could not believe what he had done. He moved away and then turned round. He still had a pistol. I stopped walking and he looked straight at me. I thought, he only has to take aim and that's me. As I walked away, he went to pick up the rifle.'

Carol Hall, David Sparrow and Michael Palmer heard the rapid fire of four or five shots from inside the swimming pool. They rushed towards the cabby to give him first aid. But they needed little medical expertise to realize that Marcus Barnard was dead. Jenny Barnard recalls: 'We had to drive past Barney's car — and my mum told me not to look. But I went and did the human thing and had to look. There were police photographers there and they had the black bag by the side of the car, and the police made us stop right behind it. And I just wanted to go to him. I think that that one image will probably haunt me for the rest of my life. But what does make me so angry is how the press gave Ryan this Rambo-like image. They portrayed him as a Rambo-type figure and thereby made him a film star. But in fact he was nothing more than a madman.'

Jenny Barnard was right. Whatever his mental state, Michael Ryan was certainly no film star. On the contrary, he was a loner, going nowhere. But there was undeniably already an uncanny resemblance developing between Ryan's bloody exploits in Hungerford and those of the violent character Rambo in the film *First Blood*, starring the American actor Sylvester Stallone. Rambo, a Vietnam veteran, is persecuted by a sheriff and decides to avenge himself on the community. He begins by killing a group of deputies in a forest before attacking a petrol station. Next, Rambo is seen firing automatic weapons in the town itself. At one stage he sets fire to a building in order to lure his enemies, including the sheriff, to a spot where he can fire at them.

The shooting of Sue Godfrey in the Savernake Forest, the attempted murder of Kakoub Dean at the Golden Arrow Service Station on the A4, the fires that raged in South View, murder on the streets of a market town — these might not be the stuff of which Hollywood movies are made, but the similarities are nonetheless striking. Not surprisingly, the newspapers were soon to exploit the 'Rambo connection'.

'Hungerford must be a bit of a Mess'

As news of Ryan's rampage spread, hundreds of journalists and photographers descended on the town. The local, national and international press, and television crews galore — before long they were all there, or on their way. Responsibility for liaising with the media fell to Chief Inspector Laurie Fray, the press officer of the Thames Valley Police. He was an experienced policeman, whose approach to working with the press had always been to be as forthright and friendly as circumstances would allow. It was a formula which had served him well.

'That has always been the way I work,' Chief Inspector Fray would later declare. 'My policy has always been to tell what I know, insofar as it is consistent with good policing. That usually stops any aggression on the part of the press. I know that these people are all under pressure from their editors, so I try to work with them rather than against them. I have always found this the best approach. But Hungerford was in a category all of its own. I shall never forget that day. I was having lunch in the mess at Kidlington. I went into our old control room and monitored the channel. They were feverishly trying to get a response from a traffic vehicle. It turned out to be Roger Brereton's. Since it was obviously a major incident, I decided to go immediately to Hungerford, blue lights all the way, since I knew there would be a lot of press interest and I had to be able to respond.

'I arrived there at 2.30pm. I tried to pre-empt press questions, but this was difficult for me because even after briefing myself I didn't really know all that much. The press were way ahead of us at that time in terms of their communications set-up. They all had cellular phones, for example, but I didn't. They also had satellite dishes installed on the back of Range Rovers and the like, with which they were able to do live broadcasts. The BBC, ITN, ITV — they all set up incredibly quickly. I told the media people that every half an hour I would return to an agreed rendezvous point to brief and update. And this I did throughout the afternoon.'

The vast majority of journalists co-operated with the press officer. But some did not. One photographer, for example, claimed to be a scene of crime officer, and as such was allowed into the house of one of Ryan's victims. He took several photographs of the body, which was covered in a mackintosh, and the next day his illegally obtained work appeared in the tabloid press. But it was impossible, because of the sheer scale of the slaughter, to protect every single scene of crime. The press was thus able to penetrate the inner cordon without much difficulty. But in so doing not only did they exploit others' grief, they also exposed themselves to considerable danger. One journalist was so appalled by the activities of certain of her professional colleagues that she registered a formal complaint: 'No one could or should be asked to stand up to the full battering-ram weight of today's tabloid press. Hammering at the front door, thirsty for a quote, slobbering for an exclusive, up against a deadline, ready to make meat out of mortals.'

Yet many were asked. And, as Jenny Barnard was soon to discover, the thirst of some journalists would prove to be truly unquenchable.

As Barney lay dead in his taxi, Ryan walked to the junction with Priory Avenue, where he shot and slightly injured a woman driving along that road. He was to inflict a far greater injury on John Storms, a washing-machine engineer out on a call but at that time stationary in his van at the junction of Hillside Road. Not a local man, Storms had been looking for Hungerford Park Farm but had got lost on a housing estate. It was there that he saw Ryan, less than forty feet away, and still armed with his Kalashnikov and his Beretta pistol.

John Storms recalls: 'I thought, that's a nice-looking gun. The man then dropped into a crouching position with both legs bent at the knee. He pointed the pistol at me with both hands holding it and at first I thought it was somebody messing about. Then there was a bang, there was broken glass, there was pain and then there was blood.'

As the driver's door window shattered, John Storms slumped on to the passenger seat. Raising his head slightly above the dashboard, he saw Ryan aiming at him again. There were two further bangs and the van shuddered.

'I whispered, "Please God, don't let me die!" The blood was pouring and I was sure he was going to kill me.'

Whether through divine intervention or Ryan's poor shot, John Storms did not die. Bob Barclay, a burly builder in his thirties, ran from his nearby house and, before Ryan's eyes, dragged the injured man, half running, half crouching, back to his garden. Having dialled for the emergency services, he set about stemming the bleeding. While Ryan's bullet missed John Storms's spinal cord by just two millimetres, it nonetheless shattered his jaw and burst his tongue, a fragment of the bullet lodging itself near to his larynx.

As the police operation gained momentum, the entire nation waited anxiously to learn of the latest developments taking place in the Berkshire town. The Prime Minister, Margaret Thatcher, holidaying in Cornwall, was kept informed on a special phone line from Downing Street. The Thames Valley Police put into motion the first steps for the creation of a casualty bureau. Appeals for voluntary nurses were broadcast on local radio.

As the killings continued — ten having died so far — Ryan appeared to be firing indiscriminately. His strategy was hardly sophisticated: anyone who happened to come within his range was a potential victim. Alison Chapman, however, already fired at by Ryan, disagrees. 'It was true that he looked brain dead when he was firing. But in some ways he must have known what he was doing,' she would later insist. 'Because just before he started firing in South View he shouted at all the children playing there to go indoors. And what was really curious was that the two other teenage girls he fired at were shot below the waist, as I was, while he aimed his gun directly at the heads of the older people.'

Seconds before being rescued from his car John Storms had heard the sound of an approaching car and still more shots. Despite his injury he was sure that this time the bullets were not aimed at him. And in this he was right. They were directed instead at Kathleen and Douglas Wainwright, in Hungerford to visit their son Trevor, one of the town's local bobbies, and his wife Jane. The Wainwrights had been looking forward to moving to Hungerford for their imminent retirement. They were less than a hundred yards from their destination, having driven from Strood in Kent, when their windscreen was suddenly shattered by two bullets from Ryan's gun as he stood on the pavement nearby.

'Automatically my husband put his foot on the brake,' Mrs Wainwright would later inform the inquest. 'As we stopped there was this man right opposite my husband's window on the pavement. I heard about six or eight shots, one after the other, bang, bang, bang. The gun was pointed at my husband's window. I heard him groan twice, I looked at him and I knew he was dead. Blood trickled down his nose and out of his mouth and he fell to one side. I knew he was dead. I also knew that I had been hit. I only felt a sting on the breast and my finger and hand though. This chap walked to the front of our car and started reloading his gun. I thought, oh my God, he's going to fire at me again — but as he was loading he was walking forwards. You might say that self-preservation took over. I took off my seat belt and opened the passenger door as quietly as I could and ran.'

PC Trevor Wainwright was off duty at the time, but as soon as he heard about the shooting incident he drove back to his home town, confident that his local knowledge would be invaluable to the specialist squads called in from outside. As yet he was ignorant of the fact that his father was dead — hit by three shots from the Beretta pistol, twice in the chest and once in the head — and that his mother had survived only by the slenderest of margins.

By a terrible irony, it would later emerge, it was PC Wainwright who had vetted Ryan when the latter wanted to modify his licence to cover the gun he used in the Hungerford massacre. He had called on his neighbour's home in November 1986 to check on his worthiness to hold a firearms certificate and on security arrangements in the house.

'It's bloody ironic,' the policeman would later admit. 'I would hate to think that I okayed a change in the licence for the gun that killed my father. But I really don't feel it's down to me because I didn't grant the licence — I merely did the checks. In fact those checks were very thorough. I knew for a fact that Ryan hadn't been in any serious trouble with the police. I also knew that he was something of a loner, but you can't hold that against anyone.'

On that occasion Ryan and Wainwright had laughed and joked together. They had done likewise once before, when Ryan had walked into Hungerford police station and announced that he had been caught by the police for exceeding the speed limit.

'I said: "What speed were you doing?" and he said: "A hundred and twelve miles per hour!" I said: "Silly sod" and we both had a laugh,' recalls the policeman.

The then Assistant Chief Constable, now Chief Constable, of Thames Valley Police, Charles Pollard, was in a grave mood that Wednesday, for he knew very well that responsibility for the entire police operation at Hungerford would ultimately fall on him, as he explains: 'I've been involved in big incidents before, so you do develop a way of thinking ahead of what you are going to do. But as I drove down to Hungerford what I wanted above all else was thinking time. Because often when you get to the centre of it all you get caught up with the tide of events and it is difficult to take a step back in order to reflect. No firearm can be issued and drawn by an officer without my personal permission, so I authorized their use before I left Kidlington. The first thing to do is always to set up an excellent communications centre — get set up, get staff in, and so on. Newbury and HQ were also using their control rooms — but my experience is that it's always better to set up on the spot. The local radio was not working, but the VHF set was. So that was where I decided to set up the operations room. I was in overall charge of the operation, with Chief Inspector Lambert heading up the firearms response — a very experienced officer. I got a competent person to man the radio, with another making a log, and my own driver making a log of everything I did. All the time I was getting information — and trying to make sense of it — but that was not at all easy.'

Assistant Chief Constable Pollard was not the only person hungry for information that afternoon. Ryan's own relatives were themselves extremely concerned to find out precisely what was happening in Hungerford. They too had been listening to the news. The gunman's cousin, David Fairbrass, explains: 'We had heard all about this mad gunman on the loose in Hungerford, and my mother was desperately trying to reach her sister Dorothy on the phone to find out if she and Michael were safe. Then we saw pictures of their burning house on the television and my mother was beside herself with worry.'

Eric Vardy was to be Ryan's twelfth victim. A carpenter and driver for Norland Nursery College, he had given up his job as a manager of a coach-building company to be closer to his wife Marlyne, who was stricken with cancer. The couple had recently celebrated their silver wedding anniversary, when Eric had presented his wife with a beautiful ring. Mr Vardy was travelling in a white Sherpa minibus with his passenger Steven Ball when they came under fire from Ryan. Immediately before driving up Tarrants Hill, the two men had seen a police car and a crowd near a public house and assumed that there had been a fight there. Oblivious to the danger, they carried on up the High Street in search of an alternative route to their destination, a builders' supplier.

Steven Ball would later describe how the van's windscreen was suddenly shattered and Eric Vardy's body 'jumped up and slumped', the vehicle then speeding off out of control before crashing next to a telegraph pole. Eric Vardy had been hit twice, just under the chin and in the side. He was to die later as a result of shock and a haemorrhage caused by the bullet wound to his neck. 'In my own heart,' his widow Marlyne would later reveal, 'I blame the police for having let his vehicle go through and not attempting to stop the traffic, or to warn them that there was a gunman on the loose.'

Nor would Marlyne Vardy be the only person to have cause to complain about the tactics of the Thames Valley Police that afternoon.

Leaving Tarrants Hill, Ryan then walked into Priory Road. It was there that he took aim at Sandra Hill, driving along that road in her red Renault 5. Taking advantage of the sunshine and clearly in good spirits, she had the window down and the car radio on loud. She had decided to take a day off from work in order to visit old friends. In an instant Ryan ensured that that day would be her last, hitting her with a single bullet fired through the open window. Graham Brunsden was one of the first helpers to reach Sandra Hill. He found the twenty-two-year-old with her mouth full of blood and a bullet wound in her chest. After he helped to remove her from the car, she was taken to a nearby doctor's surgery. She was dead on arrival — Ryan's thirteenth victim, but by no means his last.

The gunman continued down Priory Road, where he broke into number sixty, a detached house belonging to Myrtle and Victor Gibbs. Mr Gibbs, aged sixty-six and known to everyone as Jack, had a reputation as a cautious man, always going out of his way to ensure that his doors were securely locked. One blast from Ryan's Kalashnikov removed all pretence of security, and Jack soon found himself face to face in the kitchen with the gunman. Immediately, the pensioner threw himself across his wife's wheelchair to protect her from a further burst of firing, this time from the Beretta. Jack Gibbs died of multiple gunshot wounds to the chest, while his wife, already crippled with arthritis, lay critically wounded. The shots were heard by the Gibbs's next door neighbour, Mrs Sylvia Dodds, who would later describe her neighbours as 'a devoted couple wonderfully happy with one another'. In fact they had been sweethearts from their early teens. Their happiness together, which had spanned more than half a century, ended abruptly shortly after one o'clock that Wednesday afternoon when Ryan had burst in through their front door.

From the Gibbs's home, Ryan then fired at nearby houses, injuring a man at number sixty-two and a woman at number seventy-one. Both were to survive. Ian Playle, however, would not. The thirty-four-year-old was clerk to the Justices at Newbury Magistrates Courts and one of the youngest solicitors in the country to hold such a post. He had come to Hungerford with his wife, Elizabeth, and their two young children, Richard and Sarah, on a shopping trip. They had set off from their home in Newbury in their Ford Sierra before running into a police roadblock at Inkpen Gate. At that Hungerford landmark, Elizabeth Playle had at first not believed that the men standing there were detectives, but her husband soon recognized them as regular visitors to the courtrooms at Newbury. Without seeking or being given a reason for the roadblock, they sought an alternative route into the centre of Hungerford, and drove down Priory Road, rounding a sharp righthand bend.

'The car started making a whirring sound,' Elizabeth Playle would later explain, 'and I turned round to ask Ian what the matter was — and there was blood pouring from his neck — and we crashed into another car.'

One witness, one of the heroes of Hungerford that afternoon, heard from a truck driver that a little further along the road there was a family in trouble.

'There was a woman in the passenger seat holding

some kind of rag into the guy's neck,' he remembers. 'She was screaming, "He's gone, he's gone!" I asked to see the wound. There was no blood coming out and there was no pulse. She was screaming hysterically, "I'm a nurse. He's gone, he's gone. Help me. Help me. Ian, please don't die."'

Elizabeth Playle sat alongside her critically injured husband as she waited for assistance. But he was to die later from a single bullet wound to the neck from the Beretta. Ian Playle was to be the last person to receive fatal injuries at the hands of the crazed gunman of Hungerford.

Quite apart from the burden of coping with her grief, Mrs Playle, like Mrs Vardy, was not at all satisfied with the conduct of the police. She later complained that inadequate information by the police officers who stopped them on Hungerford Common had resulted in her husband entering Hungerford from another direction when, quite clearly, the Playle family should not have been entering the town at all. She would further complain of inadequate assistance from the police in tracing her children, who had become separated from her in the aftermath of the tragedy. These complaints would later be adjudicated upon by the Police Complaints Authority.

However, Mrs Playle's criticisms of the police were to cut little ice with the West Berkshire coroner, Mr Charles Hoile, who would in due course advise the inquest jury. 'We, as a nation,' the coroner declared, 'cannot have it both ways. We cannot insist on having an unarmed police force and at the same time expect the police force in an emergency of this sort to become armed and be available at the drop of a hat. We have got to pay for the privilege of having the police force which is on our side, not threatening us. It is an important part of our liberty, which most people would be very reluctant to do away with. Aside from the question of the armed officers, the police response was obviously pretty prompt.'

Not prompt enough for George Noon though. Because, as Ryan made his way towards the John O'Gaunt School, he shot and injured Mr Noon as he stood in the garden of his son's house at 109 Priory Road, wounding the sixty-seven-year-old in the shoulder and eye. As George Noon lay critically injured, however, his son Tim was being spreadeagled and frisked by police. The armoured Land Rover, summoned earlier by Chief Inspector Lambert, had driven through the hedge and pulled up at the door of the Noon household. Tim, explains: 'There must have been twenty police with pistols or machine-guns pointing straight at me. My sister Sue came downstairs as they came in and we were both given the once-over and searched. I heard one policeman say, "Shall I put him in handcuffs?" I kept trying to explain that I was not the gunman and that my father had been shot.'

By a little after 1.45pm, the police helicopter had arrived and was circling above the town. It had been delayed fifteen minutes for repairs. On board was a police marksman, although his weapon was just a shotgun — clearly no match for Ryan's Kalashnikov. The helicopter was therefore obliged to land again, ten minutes later, to pick up a rifle for the marksman as soon as it had been delivered. As the helicopter swooped and searched, Ryan was still heading towards the school.

Three doors away from the Noons, Bert Whatley saw Ryan approach the rear of the school. It was shortly before 2pm. 'He was walking up the road and turned into the school premises,' Mr Whatley would later explain. 'He had his head held down very, very low — you could just see the back of his neck — he didn't turn round and he was walking very slowly, and he had a handgun in his left hand, heading to the ground, and a rifle over his right shoulder.'

Sergeant Paul Brightwell was now also in action. Chief Inspector Lambert had tasked him, together with his party of police constables, to investigate the school. Neither Lambert nor Brightwell knew at that time that this was indeed the correct location. What Sergeant Brightwell did know, however, was that his handgun, a standard police-issue .38 Smith and Wesson, a six-shot revolver, was not in the same league as Ryan's semi-automatic rifle.

'I wasn't thinking of my family then. I was just thinking one thing: where is he? By now we were very much on our toes. We got called in for a quick briefing by Mr Lambert at Hungerford police station and the name Michael Ryan was given to us. There were lots of people, lots of information. I was given a map — because obviously I didn't know Hungerford and headed off towards the school.'

Other parties went elsewhere. Heading up his party, Sergeant Brightwell had a handgun, as did all his constables apart from two who had pump-action shotguns.

'It was simple, in one sense. "Here's a map. You're here. The school's there. Now off you go." We deployed on foot, very slowly, stalking either side of the road. You are looking around you all the time. We just didn't know where this bloke was. I was in the middle of the party, trying to listen to the radio, and relying upon my blokes to keep their eyes open. He could have been anywhere. I had to concentrate on the map and the radio. We walked slowly. It must have taken us an hour. At one point we got held up at Bulpit Lane. One of my PCs sighted someone in a house in a camouflage jacket. Since this partly fitted the description of the suspect it obviously couldn't be ignored. But that person was eliminated and on we went. I just kept on thinking that I had to get to that school.'

During that bloody afternoon, shots were heard coming from South View. It would later emerge that this was part of Ryan's arsenal exploding, ignited by the flames. But since it could have been the gunman it had to be investigated. And then other sightings would be reported. As Sergeant Brightwell's party advanced, people would pop up from their gardens and out of windows, giving their views on where the gunman had headed. But much of the information continued to be either inaccurate or out of date, or in some cases, both.

'We then found poor old George Noon,' Sergeant Brightwell would later report. 'He had been shot in the head. People were comforting him. We tried to get him out because he was in a bad way. I spoke to Mr Lambert about getting him out, but he decided that it was too risky to send any ambulances in until we knew where Ryan was. As we continued to advance, though, I had a hunch that we might well be on the right track.'

Shadowing the Tactical Firearms Team as they went about their task were certain members of the press corps, jeopardizing their own lives and indeed the entire police operation. On more than one occasion Sergeant Brightwell had to forcibly evict them from the area.

'We finally arrived at the school. But we still didn't know that he was there. My job was to contain the front and sides of the school as best I could, knowing that there was another party covering the back of the school. But there was a vast open expanse around the school, so that containment was not easy. I was reporting to Mr Lambert, but I knew he was getting so much information, I just told him that we had arrived and were OK. He sent down one of his inspectors to see how our containment was. All the time, the helicopter was around and about.'

Chief Inspector Lambert had based himself in a Portakabin outside Hungerford police station, and from there established his firearms control, maintaining radio contact with each team as they went about their allotted tasks. But as the minutes became hours, he grew extremely concerned that there was still no definitive sighting of Ryan.

'I kept thinking,' the Chief Inspector would later recall, 'why the hell haven't we found him yet? Why the hell hasn't the helicopter spotted him? If he was moving about, as many of the reports would have had us believe, then it was almost certain that he would have been seen by the helicopter. Once the two other teams had dealt with their enquiries, I sent them off to join Sergeant Brightwell's party at the school. Altogether they had had to check out eight erroneous reports. Many had been panic-stricken; one even turned out to be a car backfiring.'

At 5.26pm Ryan was spotted at a window of the school. Immediately Hungerford was declared safe for the waiting ambulances, although some earlier rescue work had been carried out by the armoured Land Rovers. It had taken the police four and three-quarter hours to pinpoint Ryan after they had first received notice of him.

'I think that that must have been the biggest feeling of relief that I have ever experienced,' Chief Inspector Lambert explains. 'Because once I had made sure that the containment of the school was absolutely tight, I then knew full well that he wasn't going to be going anywhere.'

For the next ninety minutes or so, Ryan and Sergeant Brightwell were to have a long and detailed conversation. From the point of view of the police, these protracted negotiations had just one objective: Ryan's surrender.

'Hungerford must be a bit of a mess,' the gunman shouted.

11.
Emergency

Shortly before two o'clock that afternoon, nursing sister June Fawcett walked into the waiting room of the Accident and Emergency department of Swindon's Princess Margaret Hospital. Less than ten minutes later the waiting room had been cleared. The reason for the hasty evacuation was quite simple: having been alerted to Ryan's rampage through Hungerford, the department was to receive four casualties within the next few minutes. And with Berkshire's ambulance service warning that there were many more to follow, the nurse was well aware that there would be no time to deal with the more familiar workload of cuts, bruises, fractures and sprains.

One Bloody Afternoon

Situated some fifteen miles from Hungerford, the Princess Margaret was the nearest hospital with an Accident and Emergency department equipped to cope with the situation. Although the Princess Margaret, Swindon's district hospital, had 400 beds, the department was then able to take only fourteen stretcher patients. It consisted of a resuscitation room, two minor operating theatres and a number of cubicles. Attached to it was an eleven-bed observation ward, manned by Accident and Emergency department personnel.

Although some nurses had experience of shotgun wounds, none had experience of those caused by the high-velocity bullets of a semi-automatic rifle. Staff were shortly to discover that whereas a shotgun causes a peppering effect, the damage caused by the bullet of a Kalashnikov is more likely to lead to extensive internal damage and in many cases to large exit wounds.

The massacre had begun during the hospital's afternoon shift overlap, which meant that a few more staff were on hand than might otherwise have been the case. Soon the two nursing sisters, three staff nurses, four enrolled nurses and seven third-year student nurses were to face what must surely be the ultimate test for any Accident and Emergency unit anywhere: to provide a medical response to widespread and gratuitous slaughter. Medical personnel already present at the department that afternoon consisted of a senior house officer, a local

GP working as a clinical assistant and a student of medicine. They too were to be put through their paces.

In fact the hospital's service manager was already in action, informing the X-ray department, alerting the blood bank and, anticipating the grim outcome of Ryan's rampage, contacting the hospital's chaplain. As appeals went out for extra doctors and support staff to report for duty, routine admissions were cancelled. It was imperative that there should be sufficient beds to accommodate the injured. Before long, the hospital was buzzing with an atmosphere of busy efficiency.

June Fawcett's diary notes:

'14.15. An unconscious fifty-two-year-old male with a gunshot wound to the neck arrives and is taken straight into the resuscitation room.

'14.19. Another call from ambulance control; two more casualties with serious gunshot wounds are on the way.

'14.20. The casualties with gunshot wounds arrive; a thirty-seven-year-old male with an injury to his left upper arm, a sixty-two-year-old female with injuries to her left hand and right side of chest, and a forty-nine-year-old male wounded in the throat and lower mandible. All are able to walk into the department. Quickly assessing them, I allocate nurses to initiate their care and treatment. The man with facial injuries requires the attention of the faciomaxiliary team, who are immediately summoned.'

And so it was to continue throughout that afternoon and early evening, as Ryan's victims eventually arrived at the Princess Margaret, some having waited a considerable time.

One young man in Hungerford that afternoon was not prepared to stand idly by waiting for the arrival of the emergency services. For Lance Corporal Carl Harries, a veteran of the Falklands War despite his twenty-one years of age, was a man of action. For almost an hour and a half the off-duty soldier, at that time serving with the Royal Engineers at Maidstone in Kent, was to repeatedly risk his life feverishly running around the town tending to one victim after another.

'I was walking into town to pick up a radiator hose,' the soldier would later recall, 'when I heard gunshots. I thought someone was just messing around. Then suddenly I saw this guy standing in front of me, dressed in US-style combat gear and headband, looking like Rambo. He had a pistol in his hand and an automatic weapon slung over his shoulder. I dived through a hedge and stayed low for one or two minutes. But as I scrambled out I heard rapid gunfire.'

The gunfire heard by Harries was directed at Sandra Hill, who was driving into Hungerford on her day off from work.

'I saw this car, engine running, radio blaring, still moving slowly along the road. There was a bullet hole in the windscreen and a young woman slumped at the wheel. She tried to speak, but her mouth and throat were full of blood. I tried desperately to clear her mouth, but it was useless — I knew she was dying.'

His hands still covered in blood, Harries was then alerted to the fact that a man had been shot through the neck in a Ford Sierra. It was Ian Playle, the clerk to the Justices at Newbury Magistrates Courts, seeking a way into Hungerford.

'I tried mouth-to-mouth and chest compresses and he started breathing again. His pulse came back, but then the blood started pumping out of his neck. Then I heard a noise from a house across the road. I looked through the letter-box and saw a man cowering behind the door. He had been shot in the knee. He told me that he was OK, but that there had been another shooting next door. I ran over and found that the lock had been blown off the door and the glass partition kicked in. Mrs Gibbs, who lived there, must have heard the crunch of glass under my feet and called for help. There was blood everywhere. She was screaming by her husband's side. I could tell he was already dead: his eyes were fixed in a death stare.'

While the courageous soldier was in search of victims to see what assistance he might be able to render, his father, Peter Harries, was looking for his son, having heard that he had been trailing the gunman. I was frantic,' Peter Harries would later admit. 'I thought, Christ, he could be killed. I have to come to terms with that — he's a soldier. But abroad, yes; in your home town in Berkshire, no. When I eventually caught up with him he was crying. I just broke up too.'

Lance Corporal Harries would later receive the Queen's Commendation for Brave Conduct. For a little over ninety minutes he had cradled the dying and heard their last words. He comforted the wounded and covered up those for whom there could be no help. Or, as the Queen's citation would put it: 'Without consideration for his own safety Lance Corporal Harries continued to render first aid to the injured and dying both in the street and in their houses and to organise members of the public in this task.'

The doctors and nurses of the Princess Margaret Hospital had been trained to control their emotions. Not that they were in any sense immune to the enormity of the tragedy in which they had become key players. It was just that their training had taught them otherwise. Before long a consultant anaesthetist from the intensive care unit had arrived, an incident room had been set up in the department manned by both police and the hospital's administrative staff, and inevitably the coroner's officer had made contact too.

Among those to visit the injured at the hospital was the Reverend David Salt. Aware that it was his responsibility to comfort the bereaved and to offer support, he had himself been praying for extra strength.

'I have to say that my visit to the hospital at Swindon was a unique experience,' he explains. 'You would have thought that they had just had a ward party; there were balloons everywhere. They were almost on a high, I would say. It was perhaps because of all the media attention, although I couldn't be sure. Often that can help because it can make you feel that you are not alone. What I do know, though, is there was very much a feeling of thankfulness that they were alive. There was a tremendous camaraderie on that ward. There was no wailing. Even by the poor lady who had lost her husband, Mrs Wainwright. I came with the heavy task of comforting these people, but their calmness and fortitude were quite unexpected.'

At 4pm the RAF hospital at nearby Wroughton made contact with the Accident and Emergency department of the Princess Margaret, informing staff there that it was in a position to take the next two serious and six minor casualties. It was a generous offer, designed to relieve the pressure building up at the Swindon hospital, and it was gratefully accepted. Betty Tolladay, the elderly lady who had been shot after rebuking Ryan about the noise he had been making, finally found her way there. Of all those injured in the massacre, it was Betty Tolladay who had been the most closely involved in David Salt's congregation at St Lawrence's. One of those seriously injured, she was now to face a series of operations.

In Hungerford, medical staff from the town's surgery treated the injured who had been brought there, while doctors went out with police in a series of search-and-rescue missions, some of them then accompanying the wounded on their journey to the Princess Margaret Hospital. Meanwhile, in Newbury, news of the incident was reaching the divisional social services offices. Immediately, the Director of Social Services was informed, as were the county's Emergency Planning Officer and the press officer at Shire Hall, Reading. The bureaucratic machinery, used to proceeding at a more leisurely pace, nonetheless swung into action at once, the Housing Department of Newbury District Council soon standing by to accommodate those made homeless as a result of Ryan's razing of part of South View.

Hazel Haslett, the ambulancewoman who had braved Ryan's hail of bullets to rescue the injured, was herself treated at the Princess Margaret that afternoon, having been showered with glass from her ambulance windscreen and receiving leg and arm injuries. She and Linda Bright, the driver, would later be commended for their bravery, for, putting their own suffering to one side, they would continue to work late into the night.

While Haslett and Bright ferried the injured to safety, eight surgeons were operating on twelve patients. But although the hospital's assistant general manager, Paul Vandendale, was eventually able to confirm that the progress of the majority of his patients was 'satisfactory', Myrtle Gibbs, Ian Playle and George Noon all remained in critical condition in intensive care. At the Accident and Emergency department, there was consequently a continuous updating of information, as orthopaedic consultants and registrars liaised with anaesthetists to discuss the progress and prospects of this patient or that.

Twenty-five miles from Hungerford, in Calne, Wiltshire, the unease in the Fairbrass household had by now reached breaking-point. Michael Ryan's relatives were still desperate to find out if he and his mother had survived the massacre. Then, suddenly, the BBC's mid-evening news bulletin put them in the picture. It was not at all what they had been expecting to hear.

'All the time my mother was extremely worried,' Ryan's cousin, David Fairbrass, would later recall. 'Because my mother and her sister Dorothy were extremely close. Then, on the *Nine O'Clock News*, they named Michael as the killer. We were stunned. There was total disbelief. Who could accept such a thing?'

The Drinkwater family, then holidaying in France, were shortly to be stunned too. Linda and Kevin Drinkwater, together with their two young children, had left for a touring holiday in France on Tuesday, 18 August, the day before Michael Ryan was to change the character of the town of Hungerford for all time. Their home in South View, recently purchased from the council, was one of the row of four cottages he set on fire. French police had been informed of the particulars of the Drinkwaters' vehicle so that they could be alerted to the tragedy, but to no avail. Linda Drinkwater explains: 'We didn't know anything about it until we got on to the ferry and we read it in the newspaper. Just at the bottom of one article it said that we were on holiday — something like "they were on holiday in France and are unaware that their house has burnt down". When we eventually did make it back home, all that was left was the video in the living-room.'

After recovering from the initial shock of losing his home, along with his business van parked outside, Kevin Drinkwater was soon able to put the family's loss in perspective: 'We were in the luckiest place — as far away from Hungerford as possible. Had we been here, anything could have happened. I could have been going to my wife's funeral. Anything. Somebody was looking over us that week, that's for definite. Because we still have our children. Everything we have lost can be replaced. The dead cannot.'

Although staff at the Princess Margaret Hospital were acting speedily and professionally, the massacre was not sufficiently severe, according to the hospital's own rules and regulations, to be designated a major incident. The district plan had defined a major incident as one involving twenty or more stretcher cases. Senior hospital nurse Anne Eggleton, in charge of the emergency unit on the day of the tragedy, was well aware that if ever anything constituted a major incident, it was Ryan's slaughter of the innocent in Hungerford. But she also knew that rules were rules, drafted by wise committees whose members had ostensibly considered these things. In any event, Anne Eggleton had other worries on her mind than juggling with statistics. Aware that ambulance personnel had come under fire, she was worried that her own husband might be among the injured: 'My husband Stephen was on duty at Hungerford that day and I realized what was going on. I had no contact with him until he came home late at night.'

Nonetheless the atmosphere within Anne Eggleton's department, although tense, continued to be based on excellent rapport between the staff, and a first-class team spirit pervaded the entire unit. Every now and then, there would be the odd humorous exchange. To the outsider, these might have sounded callous and uncaring. But among the nurses and doctors working at the hospital they served a useful role, providing an outlet for anxiety and tension. It was not until seven o'clock that evening that ambulance control was finally able to report that no more casualties would be sent to the Princess Margaret. The immediate pressure was over. And the Accident and Emergency department had passed its most rigorous test with flying colours.

Over the next few days there was to be both good news and bad at the Princess Margaret Hospital. Lisa Mildenhall, for example, Ryan's youngest victim, was

making a rapid recovery and soon found herself able
to celebrate a family birthday in hospital. Mrs Myrtle
Gibbs, on the other hand, was never to regain
consciousness. Ever since her admission, she had only
been able to breathe with the assistance of a life-
support machine. One of her four sons, then serving
with the RAF in Denmark, was flown to the hospital
by helicopter and was with her when she died.
Another son was being flown back from overseas
when news of his mother's death was broken to him
in mid-flight. The neighbours were unanimous in
their judgement: Mrs Gibbs would not have wanted
to live without her husband, who had died
courageously trying to save her.

A few hours after Mrs Gibbs's death, staff at Ian
Playle's office in the Magistrates Courts in Newbury
broke down and wept on being informed that Ian,
who had been transferred to Oxford's John Radcliffe
Hospital, had also died. He was Ryan's sixteenth and
final fatality.

Mr Charles Hoile, the West Berkshire coroner,
would later pay tribute to the heroism and courage of
the people of Hungerford. What had happened, he
would inform the inquest jury, was absolutely
unprecedented not just in one remote corner of
Berkshire but in the whole of Britain. 'It is a matter,'
he would declare, 'which has held the whole nation in
horrified fascination.'

And at no time was this horror and fascination
more intense than when the news media reported that

Ryan had disappeared into the John O'Gaunt School, where he had been a pupil a little over a decade earlier. For a few hours, there had been no more shootings in Hungerford, and an eerie silence had descended over the town. The sound of gunfire had ceased, the smell of cordite had begun to fade. But the gunman, it seemed, now had something to say.

12.
'I Killed all those People'

The John O'Gaunt School, Hungerford's uninspiring redbrick comprehensive, offered from its third storey a wide, unrestricted view of the town. It was there that Ryan had chosen to position himself. Fortunately, the school was closed, its pupils away for the long summer holidays. The caretaker, however, was in his bungalow beside the school, with his two children. A phone call from his wife from her place of work had warned him of the shootings.

'The next thing I knew,' John Miles would later explain, 'two terrified kids came riding up the road on bicycles shouting, "There's a man with a gun."' Rushing out to alert some workmen outside the school bungalow, Mr Miles had noticed a man in army fatigues walking up the drive. It was Ryan. 'My kids and I crouched behind the bushes with the workmen. We could see him but he could not see us.'

Unlike Bert Whatley, who had earlier dialled 999 to inform the police that Ryan was at the school — only to find the telephone exchange overwhelmed with calls — John Miles managed to get through on his third attempt. Since he was himself a former policeman, the Thames Valley Police immediately treated his information extremely seriously. Nonetheless, there remained a number of other reported sightings to be investigated and it would clearly have been reckless of the police to have suddenly abandoned these. Unfortunately, one consequence of this combination of caution and confusion was that some ninety minutes were to elapse before the caretaker would finally see the police arriving at the school.

The police operation was to be hindered that afternoon by other factors too, notably the presence over Hungerford of a number of press helicopters. Their noise made searching for the gunman all the more difficult and hazardous. Some airborne television crews, desperate for the right footage, even had the nerve to ask the police helicopter to get out of the way. Ryan, however, made no distinction between them, repeatedly firing at police and press helicopters alike. The Thames Valley Police eventually dealt with the airborne press corps by seeking and obtaining a flying restriction from the Civil Aviation Authority. Although normal procedural corners were cut, this curb nonetheless took some time to obtain. Thus it was fortunate for the people of Hungerford that by this stage Ryan was, as radio and television were reporting in their live broadcasts, 'holed up' at the John O'Gaunt School.

Shortly before 5pm shots were heard from the school's vicinity. Shortly after the hour another shot was heard. This time there could be no doubt: it had unquestionably come from the school. Then, a few minutes later, there was conclusive evidence of Ryan's presence in the school, for, at 5.25pm, he threw his Kalashnikov out of a third-floor window. It was the weapon with which he had killed eight people and fired eighty-four bullets. Seconds later he was seen in a classroom. But what the police did not know at that time was that Ryan was wearing a bullet-resistant waistcoat which would have protected him against all but the most powerful of police weaponry.

'There had been a bit of an impasse,' Sergeant Brightwell would later recall. 'So the next move was when we heard that single shot. Maybe he was trying to attract attention to himself, I don't know. I ran through the back gardens and went crashing over some fences to get nearer to the officer, PC Anthony Bates, who gave the report. I then saw the rifle on the pavement outside the school; it had come crashing on to the ground. One of my PCs had called out to him to make contact. He said: "You are surrounded by armed police. Do as you are told and no harm will come to you!" But we couldn't hear the reply. Still, at least we knew he was there — up on the top floor of the school. Together with the PC, I ran across the pavement to the corner of the building and then made contact with Michael Ryan, who was in one of the classrooms. I was reporting back to Mr Lambert, my boss, but you really do have to be able to act on your own initiative in such a situation. So it was me who ended up speaking to Michael Ryan. Not because I was brave in any way — just because I happened to get there first. I had plenty of back-up. Afterwards, I had to write up the conversation. I wrote it up as best as I could recall. But it wasn't word-perfect.'

Brightwell and Ryan's conversation, which was to last almost an hour and a half, began when the gunman finally confirmed that he had heard the police message that he was surrounded. But the exchange hardly seemed to get off to a promising start.

SERGEANT: What is your first name, Mr Ryan?

RYAN: It is nothing to do with you. Mind your own business.

SERGEANT: That's OK. I just want to talk to you and get you out safely. Do you understand?

RYAN: Yes, I've nothing against you.

SERGEANT: What weapons do you have with you?

RYAN: One 9mm pistol and ammunition.

SERGEANT: Mr Ryan, this is very important. Do not come to the window holding any weapons. Do you understand?

RYAN: I understand. I also have a grenade.

SERGEANT: Do not come to the window with the grenade. Do you understand?

RYAN: Yes.

SERGEANT: What type of grenade is it?

RYAN: Israeli fragmentation type.

SERGEANT: I want to get you out of the building safely.

RYAN: Yes.

SERGEANT: It is important that you do not come to the window with any weapon. Do you understand?

RYAN: Yes.

'It was a bit of a relief when I was immediately answered,' Sergeant Brightwell would later reveal. 'He was actually easy to talk to. The whole enormity of what he had done didn't dawn upon me at the time. I had met George Noon on the way down though, and seen Douglas Wainwright slumped over his car — so I knew what he had done all right. I just wanted to keep him talking — to get him out of the building, as you can see from my report. I didn't want him to be shot. That's the training. Although I'm not a proper police negotiator, we do learn how to negotiate with someone in a building as part of our overall tactical training. I was nervous but not shaking. So at this stage I switched my radio off, in order to be able to concentrate more effectively. Another PC with me was in radio contact and reporting back all the time to Mr Lambert.'

Chief Inspector Lambert, leading the Support Group, had by now moved out of his Portakabin outside Hungerford police station and headed towards the school. Accompanying him on this short journey was a trained police negotiator, expert in psychological tactics and techniques, who had been standing by for some time. But Lambert was soon satisfied that the dialogue between Sergeant Brightwell and Ryan was going well. It was his judgement that no useful purpose could be served by a sudden change of personnel. In fact he was more worried about Ryan's claim to have a grenade, so he ordered additional police armoury to cover the window of the classroom where the gunman had been seen. As the Chief Inspector continued to monitor the dialogue, he became convinced that Ryan was going to give himself up.

Just as the head of the Support Group was happy for Sergeant Brightwell to proceed with the negotiations, so the Assistant Chief Constable, Charles Pollard, was content to follow the judgement of his firearms adviser.

'While I was in overall charge of the police operation, you do have to be able to delegate,' Charles Pollard would later insist. 'So I let Paul Brightwell get on with it via Glyn Lambert. Because once I knew that we had the school contained, it became, in some respects, a routine policing matter. We now had the situation under control. It was at this stage that I too went down to the school.'

'Although the conversation went on for well over an hour,' Sergeant Brightwell would later explain, 'it seemed more like five minutes. All the time he was both lucid and calm. There were the odd gaps in the dialogue, but other than that it was almost continuous. On several occasions I really did think that he was going to make a move and come out. I knew precisely how I wanted him to come out, because of the training. But he did keep on asking about his mother.'

Altogether, Ryan would ask the Sergeant about the plight of his mother, Dorothy, well over a dozen times. Indeed it was the central theme of their conversation.

RYAN: I want to know how my mother is. Tell me about my mother.

SERGEANT: I will try to find out about your mother. Just bear with me.

RYAN: I must know about my mother.

SERGEANT: Mr Ryan, do you have any other weapons?

RYAN: I've got a .32 CZ pistol but that is in for repair. I must know about my mother. Tell me. I will throw the grenade out of the window.

SERGEANT: Don't do that. I'm trying to find out.

RYAN: That is ridiculous. You must know. I want to know.

SERGEANT: Mr Ryan, when I tell you to, I want you to stand up and look out of the window to the front of the school.

RYAN: What for?

SERGEANT: If you stand up, we will know what

door you are coming out of.

RYAN: I'm not standing up. Have you found out about my mother yet?

SERGEANT: Not yet, I'm still trying.

RYAN: I'm not coming out until I know.

'As you can see,' Sergeant Brightwell would later explain, 'he kept on asking about his mother. But I can tell you that she was as dead as a doornail. It seemed to me that by asking about her continuously he was almost trying to let himself off of the hook in some way.'

The conversation continued.

SERGEANT: I want you to leave all your weapons in that room. Do you understand?

RYAN: Yes. My pistol is tied to my wrist with a lanyard. I have one round of ammunition.

SERGEANT: Can you undo the lanyard?

RYAN: No.

'I must say that I was perplexed by this man,' Ryan's interlocutor would later admit. 'I just wanted him to do as I was telling him. I still thought that I

was going to get him out. It seemed to me as if he
wanted to come out. I was shouting because of the
distance between us. A couple of times I had to ask
him to speak up. But what he said about the gun
being tied to his wrist with a lanyard worried me.
Because I knew that if he did come out he could
easily have been shot, had the gun been
misinterpreted, for example. But he still seemed to be
happy to talk. He asked about my rank and so on. So
we carried on talking.'

SERGEANT: It is important that you come out
with no weapons.

RYAN: I had an M1 carbine which I left in the
park. It was on a gravel path near the body of a mate I
shot near the swimming pool. There should be a
thirty-round magazine with it.

SERGEANT: Thank you for that, Mr Ryan.

RYAN: Also, there is my dog. Has anybody found
that? It is a black labrador. I shot it. I had my eyes shut
the first time and I just winged it. I have undone the
lanyard. I also have body armour.

SERGEANT: Thank you. Will you come out?

RYAN: I am not coming out until I know about
my mother.

SERGEANT: I am trying to find out. But I want you to come out leaving all your weapons in the room.

RYAN: Where shall I leave them — on the window-sill?

SERGEANT: Don't come to the window holding any weapon. Just leave them on the floor. Do you understand?

RYAN: Yes.

SERGEANT: Just leave all your weapons in the room and come out.

RYAN: I will come down the stairs outside.

SERGEANT: The stairs with the rifle out in front?

RYAN: Yes, those stairs.

SERGEANT: When you come outside look to the left and you will see me. Do not make any move towards the rifle. I want you to leave your body armour in the room as well, Mr Ryan.

RYAN: Why's that?

SERGEANT: I need to be able to see you have nothing concealed, that you understand my position.

RYAN: Yes, I understand. I am not going to come out until I know about my mother.

SERGEANT: I am doing my best, Mr Ryan. I am still trying to find out about your mother. If you come out, we will be able to sort it out much quicker.

Sergeant Brightwell later explained: 'All the time I was trying to play down what he had done. To give him the impression that we could sort everything out, that I was a sort of friend who he could talk to — even though it was obvious that the bloke was completely nuts and needed locking away for the rest of his life. So when he asked about the casualty figures, I again tried to talk the whole thing down.'

RYAN: What are the casualty figures?

SERGEANT: I don't know. Obviously you know you shot a lot of people.

RYAN: Hungerford must be a bit of a mess.

SERGEANT: You are right. They know you have been through. Do you know how many you have shot?

RYAN: I don't know. It's like a bad dream.

SERGEANT: It has happened. The sooner you come out, the easier it will be to sort out.

RYAN: I know it's happened. I'm not stupid.

SERGEANT: I know that, mate.

RYAN: How's my mother? She's dead, isn't she? That's why you will not tell me. I am throwing the magazine of the pistol out. I still have one round left, though.

SERGEANT: Why do you have that?

RYAN: It is obvious, isn't it?

SERGEANT: I want to get you out safely. Don't do anything silly.

RYAN: Don't worry. I have nothing against you. You have got your job to do.

That afternoon there was another man in Hungerford with a job to do. Sergeant David Warwick, a senior firearms instructor in the Support Group, had Michael Ryan in his telescopic gun sight for a full minute. And yet he chose not to pull the trigger.

'If I had fired,' he comments, 'then I would have been a murderer. I would have been no better than him. He was unlikely to shoot anybody else. Nor was he any longer a threat to the police or the public. It was also extremely unlikely that he was going to abscond or commit other offences. You have got to have the justification before shooting someone and the justification wasn't there.'

Unaware that Sergeant Warwick's gun had been trained on him, albeit from outside the school, Ryan continued to ask about his mother.

RYAN: You must have a radio. Get on that and find out. How many people are with you?

SERGEANT: Just a couple.

RYAN: Well, get them to do it. Have you found the M1 carbine yet?

SERGEANT: They are still looking, Mr Ryan. I have passed on all the details.

RYAN: It is just that there were some kids nearby. I don't want them to find it. And what about my dog? Have you found it? Was it on the Common?

SERGEANT: Is it important?

RYAN: Yes.

SERGEANT: It is at Hungerford police station.

RYAN: Will you look after it?

SERGEANT: Of course we will.

RYAN: Will you give it a decent burial?

SERGEANT: Yes, Mr Ryan. If you come out, you can see the dog yourself.

RYAN: What about my mother? She is dead. I know she is dead. Have you found her yet?

SERGEANT: I am still waiting, Mr Ryan.

RYAN: I have picked up my gun again.

SERGEANT: Don't do that, Mr Ryan. If you come out I will find out. All you have to do is walk slowly down the stairs with your hands in the air. Have you seen anybody in the school?

RYAN: No. I am on my own. I haven't any hostages. What time is it?

SERGEANT: It is 6.24.

RYAN: If only the police car hadn't turned up. If only my car had started.

SERGEANT: Will you come out now please, Mr Ryan?

RYAN: I want to think about it. Why won't you tell me about my mother?

SERGEANT: I don't know. As soon as you come out, we'll find out together.

RYAN: I won't come out until I know. I did not mean to kill her. It was a mistake.

SERGEANT: I understand that, mate.

RYAN: How can you understand? I wish I had stayed in bed.

SERGEANT: Mr Ryan, just come down. Leave all your weapons in the room and come down.

Within the sixty seconds that Sergeant Warwick's gun was trained on Ryan, the gunman appeared at the window, apparently unarmed. Warwick wondered if it was perhaps Ryan's way of asking the police to bring about the end. But still the police marksman refused to shoot. The senior firearms instructor knew very well that if Ryan had appeared at the window with a grenade, or anything remotely resembling a grenade, or indeed if he was holding a hostage, then the police response would have been totally different. But neither of these scenarios materialized.

'All the talk was that he was going to give himself up,' Sergeant Warwick would later explain. 'He was in an empty school, having thrown one weapon out of the window — and I can tell you he wasn't going anywhere. Pulling the trigger would therefore have been entirely the wrong decision.'

Still unaware that his life had been spared by the highest standards of professional policing on the part of Sergeant Warwick, Ryan began to dwell on the consequences of giving himself up. He asked if he could be taken to London.

RYAN: Will I be treated OK?

SERGEANT: Of course you will, Mr Ryan.

RYAN: Will I go to prison for a long time?

SERGEANT: I don't know, Mr Ryan. It is not up to me.

RYAN: You must have an idea. I will get life, won't I?

SERGEANT: I don't know, Mr Ryan. You will go to prison for a long time.

RYAN: It's funny. I killed all those people but I haven't got the guts to blow my own brains out.

SERGEANT: Mr Ryan, just leave all your weapons in the room and do exactly as you are told. Don't do anything silly. Do you understand?

RYAN: What time is it?

SERGEANT: Six forty-five. What do you want to know the time for?

RYAN: I want to think about it. I am not coming out until I know about my mother.

SERGEANT: Mr Ryan, I am still trying to find out. If you come down we will be able to find out together.

There followed several minutes during which time Michael Ryan did not speak. And then, at 6.52pm, Sergeant Brightwell heard a single, muffled shot from the classroom. The gunman, who had not expressed the slightest remorse for any one of his victims, was not to speak again.

'But that was by no means the end of the matter from our point of view,' Chief Inspector Lambert would later point out. 'Had he shot the wall? Would we all get shot if we went in there? I kept an open mind and was determined not to rush it. But I did want to finish it before dark, only a couple of hours away. I thought that there could be a booby trap. We flew a helicopter past the window — but they couldn't see in. Then someone got up on to the roof. We had a dog in front of us. These are the Tactical Firearms dogs who are used to training with us. So the dog went in first for us to see what the reaction would be. If there was a person in the room the dog would have reacted. The person on the roof was using mirrors on a long pole, and he saw Ryan, who appeared to be dead. I knew that we were almost home. People then went in and saw that he was indeed dead. We then used a technique to make sure that he was not wired for explosives before we touched him — and an explosives officer took over at this point. So the body was tied up and wired up and moved to make sure that there was no booby trap. Then I went into the classroom myself and saw him. My reaction was just one of relief. That it was over.'

When members of the Tactical Firearms Team entered the classroom, they found Ryan's body slumped in a corner on the floor near a window. His back was against the wall and his 9mm Beretta pistol, hammer still cocked, remained clasped in his right hand, tied to his wrist by a bootlace. A Home Office pathologist would later confirm that Ryan had died from a single gunshot wound to the head. It had passed through his skull, shattering his brain. The bullet wound was 0.7cm at the point of entry and the skin around it blackened and as if tattooed. The bullet had fractured the skull extensively, and its heat had singed the gunman's hair.

'I went in with some others,' Sergeant Brightwell

recalls. 'The doors were barricaded. And there he was, sitting beneath the window, dead. I thought, Oh so that's who I've been talking to. I didn't feel sorry for him. I thought that's more than he would have got if he would have come out. It's probably as close as you could have got to justice, if you like. It wasn't a case of brains being splattered everywhere, as you might think. But there was blood all over his face and up the wall. When it was all over I got back to the police station and phoned home. My wife, Sandy, knows not to expect me on time, and she would have known that I would have been involved. Still, she was mightily relieved to hear from me. It was midnight when I got home. The kids were in bed. You just try to play it down a bit. I'm not the hero of Hungerford. It's just that I ended up speaking to him. I was just doing the job I was trained to do. The people of Hungerford were brave — the public and the injured. When I got there, we now know, it was all over. He had shot his last person. In any case, I had a gun and a flak jacket, and I was surrounded by eight blokes. Those who got it had nothing. The local police were unarmed — Roger Brereton and the like. So compared to what some people saw, and to what they still have to deal with, you realize that you got off lightly.'

According to one of the tabloid newspapers, soon after the announcement that Ryan had shot himself, a good number of the townsfolk of Hungerford went wild with delight. It reported that some residents living near to the school ran into the street chanting: 'The bastard's dead, the bastard's dead.' The paper claimed that children, many of whom had been ordered to hide under their beds while Ryan was on the loose, cycled up and down yelling 'Good riddance', while in the pubs of Hungerford, drinkers toasted his death. Hungerford's mourning had thus still to begin.

Ron Tarry formed a completely different impression as he walked around the town in the wake of the shootings. He explains: 'I saw people shocked and talking in hushed tones to each other. My impression was that it was largely the press and others who had rushed into the town and were drinking in the pubs. Not one resident toasted Ryan's death, and there were no signs of rejoicing. What that newspaper reported was totally untrue.'

13.
A Community in Mourning

To the people of Hungerford:

> *Satan hit the streets again*
> *In Hungerford last week*
> *And caused us all such utter pain*
> *In letting loose his freak.*
> *People wonder where was God*
> *When this event took place*
> *And seem to think it's rather odd*
> *He didn't show His face.*
> *But don't despair I beg of you*
> *For God is well aware*
> *Of what we let the devil do*

When we don't take the care
To notice all the evil roots
Or worry who the devil shoots
Until we're on his list.
All the folk that died that day
Are up in heaven now
For God has taken them away
As only He knows how
To keep them safe and free from harm
Where Satan fears to tread
Where everything is calm
And no one's ever dead.
So rest assured you broken hearts
That everything's alright
And God will mend your injured parts
With all His strength and might.
But let us learn a lesson please
To watch what's going on
And not allow bad things to squeeze
Where they do not belong.

'That poem was written by a prisoner in Brixton prison,' the Reverend David Salt would later reveal, 'and it arrived at the parish of St Lawrence during the week following the tragedy. It was one of countless communications I received at the vicarage. In fact there were so many offers of help that the vicarage soon had someone working in every room. We got a photocopier and another telephone line pretty quickly. We would prepare mini-press releases, and many of the letters we received also contained donations. They just came flooding in. But of course they all had to be dealt with. There was a tremendous spirit of co-operation. Someone came in to keep up with the press cuttings. Much of what was reported was inaccurate. Then a rumour went around that I had said that everyone should be buried in a mass grave. I used the media myself to correct this, and I sent people around the pubs to repudiate this stupid rumour. If that had got to the bereaved, can you imagine the hurt it would have caused?'

A deeply spiritual man, the Reverend Salt had a philosophy that was nonetheless pragmatic. His message was quite simple. It was that life had to go on. So when, the morning after the tragedy, the vicar was asked if the choir's rehearsal for their production of Andrew Lloyd Webber and Tim Rice's musical *Joseph and the Amazing Technicolour Dreamcoat* should continue, he immediately replied that it should. In fact one of the girls in the show was closely involved in the tragedy. She too carried on. Could it be that the prisoner-poet's assertion that 'everything's alright' was indeed the case? Not for one moment. For the reality was that in the immediate aftermath of the massacre, Hungerford was anything but all right.

As the newspapers set about preparing their headlines that Wednesday evening, a fleet of car transporters passed through the town's darkened streets. Away went Sandra Hill's Renault 5. Away went the Playles' Ford Sierra. Roger Brereton's patrol car and Douglas Wainwright's Datsun likewise soon disappeared into the night. It was as if there was an unconscious attempt to make all evidence of the afternoon's carnage disappear. The following morning, flowers began to arrive at the town hall, where the flag flew at half-mast. Around the town, there remained traces of chalk marks where Ryan's victims had fallen, with stray bullets to be found here and there.

If there was indeed an attempt to sweep away all evidence of the massacre, it was not to be successful. For the popular press had been out in force and was now able to report the tragedy in predictable style. The *Sun* proclaimed: '15 Dead and so is Mad Rambo'. In the *Daily Mail* it was 'Bloodbath on Market Day', while the *Daily Mirror* spoke of the 'Day of the Maniac'. Many photographs obtained by subterfuge were published. None of this did anything to help the feelings of the people of Hungerford. Within a few days, in the makeshift offices of the hastily established Hungerford Family Help Unit, the telephone was ringing with sad regularity. John Smith, the co-ordinator, spoke of a town on the verge of a nervous breakdown. No more cheering and chanting now.

'What we are beginning to see in Hungerford,' the head of that newly created Berkshire Social Services unit explained, 'is the manifestation of fear, helplessness, sadness, longing, guilt, shame and anger. What we have to get across is that there is nothing abnormal about this. There is bewilderment too. We do not need specialist facilities and we are trying not to make it a medical problem. But people do need reassurance and to be told it is natural to feel this way. The stiff British upper lip is, for some people, the worst thing possible.'

As a telegram of sympathy arrived from the people of San Ysidro, California, where James Huberty shot twenty-one people dead and wounded nineteen others in the McDonald's restaurant massacre of 1984, commentators began to plough through Britain's own criminal records. The events of 19 August 1987 were without doubt the most serious shooting incident ever to take place on British soil, even bloodier than when Jeremy Bamber had slaughtered five members of his family with a rifle back in September 1984.

Unused to the concept of counselling, a good many of the people of Hungerford were nonetheless desperately in need of help. Not that there is anything new about feelings of grief or disorientation in the wake of a tragedy. Indeed, the condition has acquired a jargon of its own, PTSD, post-traumatic stress disorder, being the name given to it. The symptoms vary from one individual to another, but two of its classic features are denial and the inability to communicate. Another is the paradox of 'survivor's guilt', whereby, far from feeling thankful for being alive, survivors suffer remorse at not having done anything to prevent the death of others. Or, they insist, the little they did do was simply not enough.

One Bloody Afternoon

Murder leaves behind much debris in the lives of those it has affected. Mass murder, though, is different: it succeeds in spreading that debris throughout an entire community. This is precisely what happened at Hungerford. Common symptoms are depression, insomnia, nightmares and uncontrolled crying, while children wet the bed and become terrified of strangers. Before long the doctors of Hungerford were inundated with such complaints. Not one of them had ever imagined that one day their surgeries would be overflowing with sufferers from PTSD. Yet such a day had indeed arrived.

Jenny Barnard, whose husband, Barney, had been gunned down by Ryan, reported sensations of anger and bitterness, especially during the early days: 'A few days after it happened, I just could not understand — why him? I even got to the stage where I was thinking that I could name people — it was probably irrational thinking, I know — who it could have happened to, or who it deserved to happen to. I just felt very cheated. We used to say things to one another like: "Will you still love me when I'm sixty and wrinkled?" And I got very angry and bitter thinking, well, he's not going to see me when I'm sixty and wrinkled and I won't see him.'

Like many of his fellow citizens, Ron Tarry, the Mayor of Hungerford, was also reeling in disbelief. He had witnessed the bloodshed at the very closest of quarters, yet he found the reality difficult to digest. His own house in Sarum Way was only yards from where one victim had been gunned down, but still he struggled to believe what had happened. How on earth was it possible, he wondered, for the name of his beloved home town, with its unique and time-honoured traditions, and where he had lived peacefully since the end of the war, to have suddenly become synonymous with the very worst images of carnage and slaughter?

'I had no idea that I was going to have this role of appearing on the television thrust upon me,' Ron Tarry explains. 'The first question I was asked on TV was, what about a tragedy fund? To be honest, I hadn't even thought about a tragedy fund at that stage. We are a small community of 5,000 people where everyone knows everyone — so we were all affected. But I said that people don't want the knowledge that a tragedy fund is going to be set up; what they need is immediate help from their family and neighbours. I said that for the moment at least, money was not the priority. That was my gut reaction and, looking back, I think it was the right one. Nonetheless, the financial side of things obviously had to be addressed. And on the Thursday morning people from the Round Table made contact and said that they had some money immediately to hand — and what should they do with it? We all went to the police station. They said not to visit the families, to leave that to the social services, who are better trained at that sort of thing. But the Round Table said that they would pay for taxis, rent, TV rentals and so forth — with no red tape. I can tell you that to a lot of people that was very helpful during those first few days.'

The town council of Hungerford could hardly boast an impressive administration. Its only salaried employee was Mrs Fowler, a clerk from Newbury, and she was part-time at that. Yet members of the council gathered spontaneously at the town hall, the focal point of the town. They had come to decide what should be done. The British public, however, had already made up its mind.

'Before we had even asked for money,' the former mayor recalls, 'cheques and cash, some from children, began to arrive at the town hall. It just poured in. It was frenetic, chaotic there. But it became clear that there was going to be a need for a great deal of money, because no one was going to be able to claim on their insurance, and the Criminal Injuries Compensation Board wouldn't give a lot of money and in any case the little they do give can take a year or two to arrive. People came in with cheques for several thousands of pounds. So we decided to open a Tragedy Fund. Barclays, Lloyds and NatWest, the three banks in the town, co-operated in setting it up.'

Immediately, Peter de Savary, the financier who owns the nearby Littlecote House theme park, where Ryan had once worked for a few months as a labourer, contributed £10,000. Gareth Gimblett, the chairman of Berkshire County Council, made a personal contribution of £1,000, the local authority itself adding a further £4,000. Pensioners wrote in with smaller contributions: £1 here, £5 there. Hungerford's twin town of Le Ligueil, near Tours in France, wasted no time organizing a campaign of support.

Three trustees of the Tragedy Fund were appointed who lived in the area although not in Hungerford itself and were therefore able to take a more objective view than those closely involved in the tragedy.

Following a message of condolence from Buckingham Palace, Her Majesty's private secretary wrote to Mayor Tarry on 26 August, enclosing a personal contribution from the Queen.

Interrupting her Cornish holiday, Mrs Thatcher was soon on the scene. After flying from RAF St Mawgan in Cornwall to RAF Lyneham in Wiltshire, the Prime Minister drove the ten miles to the Princess Margaret Hospital. Having toured the streets of Hungerford and met some of the relatives of Ryan's victims, she was close to tears. Looking grave and shaken after these encounters, she spoke to the assembled members of the press. 'I am glad I have come,' she said. 'I had to come. It was so unbelievable and the only thing I could do was to be with the people who have suffered. I feel rather like most other people. There are no words in the English language which could adequately describe what happened.'

While the Prime Minister was preparing for her visit to Hungerford that Thursday, the Reverend Salt was preparing for Holy Communion at St Lawrence's.

Reading from the Book of Wisdom, he too struggled to find words which might give some comfort to the bereaved: 'The souls of the just are in God's hands and torment shall not touch them ... Their departure was reckoned as defeat and they are going from us a tragedy. But they are at peace.'

The vicar was not to struggle, however, to find words of praise for the role of the Prime Minister: 'I am someone who does not normally have many good things to say about Maggie. I used to think of her as being brash and tub-thumping. But that day she was not Maggie the politician; she was Maggie the human being. Whilst she met with the bereaved, I took Denis around the garden. I was criticized at the time for not being at the door to meet the PM. I said: "So what – the people who matter here are the bereaved."'

A few days later Downing Street was again in touch with the vicar:

Dear Mr Salt,

Thank you for inviting me to your home and enabling me to meet some of the families who lost their loved ones in the dreadful and tragic shootings at Hungerford. I appreciate the tremendous burdens on you at present, and I know that my own visit added to them. I know so well how little words can do at times like this, but if my visit helped in any way at all I am more than grateful.

My thoughts and prayers will be with you as you continue your work to help and comfort the families who are suffering so much. Yours sincerely

Margaret Thatcher

Mrs Thatcher also wrote to the Mayor:

Dear Mr Mayor

I am most grateful to you for allowing me to visit Hungerford and for accompanying me on Thursday. I was glad to be able to thank so many of those in the town who risked their lives to protect local people during those dreadful and tragic shootings. Hungerford will never forget that day. But I also know from my visit that the magnificent response of its people, and the depth of their feeling and concern for all those who have been injured or lost their loved ones will never be forgotten either. I feel for you and all those in Hungerford as you care for those who suffer, and as you face the future together. My thoughts and prayers are with you.

Yours sincerely

Margaret Thatcher

Ron Tarry was in no doubt that the Prime Minister's visit had helped a great deal: 'We were delighted that she had taken the trouble to come. I was with her throughout. I was really stunned by her, absolutely stunned. I had previously seen her as a strident parliamentarian — and she was in fact a mother, a woman interested in people and how they had suffered. I was impressed beyond words. She was very kind to the families. It was not a question of a photo-opportunity. It was just me, the local MP Michael McNair-Wilson, Denis Thatcher, the PM and the vicar. It was not a showpiece at all, because all of this took place on the lawn at the back of the vicarage. She talked about looking to the future and was superb. I had met the PM at the police station, and naturally I was keyed up. She asked me to join her cavalcade on the way to the ambulance station. My car was elsewhere, so I said we should walk, since it was only 150 yards away. Michael McNair-Wilson seemed to find the walk difficult, since he had been having dialysis. The PM was not walking with Mr McNair-Wilson but had driven on and was waiting at the ambulance station. I was, however, amazed that she noticed what I hadn't — that he didn't feel well — and she expressed concern about it. When we followed her around the fire station someone yelled that she should do something to stop people having guns so easily available, and that was the first time in Hungerford that I heard her Parliamentary voice — it was her Prime Minister's Question Time voice! But all in all it was a very moving experience. I was very emotional about the whole thing.'

Well received as it was, the Prime Minister's visit to Hungerford was such that any comfort she might have been able to provide was of a transitory nature. Longer-term care was the responsibility of the Newbury division of Berkshire County Councils Social Services. Its director, Sue Lane, had been

involved in the tragedy almost from the outset. This
was because her department was responsible for the
running of the Chestnut Walk old people's home,
outside of which somebody had been killed. In fact
two of her staff had risked their lives by rushing
outside in an attempt to help, but only to be
instructed to take cover again. Sue Lane's advice was
of an eminently practical nature: 'Don't bottle up
your feelings. Talk to your children and allow yourself
to be part of a group of people who care. Try to take
time out to sleep and rest and think, and be with your
close family and friends. And remember that there are
a lot of people who want to share and help.'

By Friday, 21 August, two days after the tragedy,
the sharing and helping to which she had referred was
to hand in the form of the Hungerford Family Help
Unit. Initially based in the town hall, this was able to
draw on support from a wide-ranging combination of
statutory and voluntary agencies, including social
workers, psychiatrists, doctors, the Victim Support
Unit, the Samaritans and the widows' charity
CRUSE. The precise purpose of the Unit was to
provide an immediate response for people in distress,
taking account of both practical and emotional needs,
in addition to the planning of continuing care and
counselling services over an extended period. Soon
leaflets outlining the Unit's role were being printed in
preparation for circulation to every Hungerford
household. That Friday afternoon and evening,
within just a few hours of its inception, social workers

started visiting families of the bereaved and those with a member who had been injured. Although the social services deserve to be complimented for acting with such rapidity, by-passing many a bureaucratic procedure, their work was not always appreciated by all. The Reverend Salt explains: 'People didn't always liaise that easily. Ron Tarry and I would try and sort them out every now and then. What we didn't want was a lot of bureaucracy being set up. And I have to say that at least half the people who were supposed to be helping were running around helping the wrong sort of people. I went into the social services offices once, to find out the addresses of relatives. All I wanted to do was to carry out my pastoral role, providing comfort and so on. But when I would be told that this information was confidential, this would really make me spit and see red.'

The Home Secretary, Douglas Hurd, found his way to Hungerford on the Sunday after the tragedy. He announced that he had already summoned a meeting of senior Home Office officials to examine the whole question of private individuals keeping weapons at their homes. There was also talk of introducing an amnesty for illegally held firearms. 'We are also considering,' he said, 'the issue of allowing civilians to have automatic and semi-automatic weapons.'

While the Home Secretary was deliberating on the issue, however, more than a dozen arms dealers from Dorset to Gateshead continued to advertise for sale, in leading gun magazines, versions of the Soviet-designed Kalashnikov assault rifle and American M1 carbine used by Ryan. In fact, Mick Ranger, the sole UK importer of the type 56 semi-automatic sold to Ryan, and who dealt directly with its Chinese manufacturers, Norinco, reported that sales of the Kalashnikov had increased significantly during the week following the massacre. He insisted that this was entirely coincidental. Nonetheless, he had sold an additional twelve such weapons since Ryan's rampage through Hungerford.

If some time was still to pass before such weaponry was outlawed, then there was considerably less hesitation about the withdrawal of gratuitously violent videos from public sale. Yet two days after the massacre Martins Newsagents in Hungerford High Street was continuing to display videos such as *Annihilation*, *Wheels of Fire* and *Wanted Dead or Alive*, all depicting violent action on their covers. While the shop's manager continued to insist that he was obliged to wait for instructions from head office before being able to remove them, the Cannon Cinema in Newbury acted on its own initiative, withdrawing the latest Mel Gibson film, *Lethal Weapon*.

It was the same story at national level too. The BBC postponed the screening of certain programmes with a violent content. Michael Grade, the then controller of programmes, announced that the three episode serial *The Marksman*, starring David Threlfall as a father hunting his son's killers, was to be delayed for several months. A New Zealand film, *Battletrack*, about a futuristic marauding gang, was likewise postponed by BBC2. It did not escape the attention of some, however, that it was the BBC which had paid £800,000 for the Rambo film *First Blood*, and that it was Michael Grade himself who had presided over its screening in September 1986. Everybody, it now seemed, was beginning to learn some lessons from Hungerford.

On the Sunday after the massacre representatives of the three religious denominations associated with Hungerford offered words of comfort to the afflicted town. Each battled hard to reconcile the random massacre with belief in God. The Reverend Salt was well aware that the eyes of the world would be firmly focused upon him that day: 'On that particular Sunday I knew there would be a lot of press interest. So I thought I might have to be a little bit careful as to what I said. But something would just shoot out of a biblical text. That hasn't happened to me since the tragedy. I was just so busy that I simply didn't have time to sit down and meditate. And yet it just flowed. It is God-given. You are just given the additional strength. In fact the best sermons always come out of your actual pastoral situations.'

Among the passages chosen for the day in the Alternative Service Book was II Timothy, Chapter 1, verse 7: 'God has not given us a spirit of timidity, but a spirit of power, and love, and self-control' Psalm 34, verse 18, reminded parishioners and press alike that:

'God is near to the broken-hearted and saves those who are crushed in spirit.'

'Humanity produces Adolf Hitler and Idi Amin as well as Mother Theresa and Martin Luther King,' the vicar went on to tell more than 300 people who crowded his parish church to overflowing. 'God gives us the power to do good and the power to do evil. God respects us as his sons and daughters and gives us freedom of choice. The events of last Wednesday leave us numb and empty. We mourn those that have been killed and grieve with those who still suffer, whether physically or mentally. I think all of us feel weak and helpless and we come before God asking for His help and healing.'

A church assistant, Mrs Trudi Pihlens, then read out a slow litany of the names of all sixteen victims. After a momentary pause, she added: 'Michael Ryan: may God have mercy on his soul.'

In Hungerford's Roman Catholic church, Father Tim Healey was likewise asking a series of questions to which he was quite unable to provide any answers.

'What are we to think — that God did not love these people? To think that is to suppose that God did not love His own Son. To conclude that their deaths were devoid of meaning and purpose is to suppose that the death of Christ is devoid of meaning. Can we say that God lost control of events last Wednesday? This would be to deny that God is God.'

The Church of Our Lady of Lourdes stands in Priory Road, where Ryan killed four of his victims.

The priest was clearly shaken by the sheer proximity of the killings, saying: 'We all acknowledge that we live in a somewhat violent society but we never believed events such as these could come so very close. Thus it was that death and injury was to visit and stalk even the very road in which this our small church is situated. It is a nightmare from which we want to wake up.'

The Superintendent Minister of the Newbury and District Methodist Church, the Reverend David Hawkes, addressed himself, by contrast, to Michael Ryan's state of mind: 'Such are the impossible questions that plague us and would undermine our struggling faith. But surely no one would want to suggest that Michael Ryan was anything but insane at the crucial moment, and a berserk mind is as much a natural.'

While the churchmen were having their say, Michael Stewart was preparing to have his. The Co-ordinator of the Bradford Fire Disaster had travelled down to Hungerford to see if he might be able to help. In fact he helped a great deal, and his talk at St Lawrence's Church entitled 'Sharing the Experiences and Problems after a Tragedy' was particularly well received. He was anxious to ensure that the lessons learned at Bradford were passed on without delay, and he did his best to encourage people to think of the longer term.

Don Philip, however, a social worker with Newbury District Council, made an important distinction between the events in Hungerford and the football-stadium fire at Bradford and the sinking of the *Herald of Free Enterprise* off Zeebrugge, which had taken place a few months earlier: 'They were terrible accidents. Whereas this incident had an element of evil. One problem which we have to face here is that whereas people were looking for scapegoats in the other disasters, here they haven't got anything other than a corpse to blame.'

And it was certainly true that to many people the crazed gunman was indeed nothing more than an evil corpse. Not to his relatives, however, for whom matters were far more complex. Ryan's cousin, David Fairbrass, explains: 'We feel mixed emotions about what happened. My own feeling is that he was sick. No normal person would do that sort of thing. My mother is a victim as well. We are all victims. Life won't be the same again. This will always stay with us.'

In the Fairbrass household there was an atmosphere of stunned silence and disbelief. Although they had first heard Ryan's name mentioned on the BBC's nine o'clock news bulletin, they had not been informed officially that their relative was indeed the perpetrator of the massacre until two o'clock the following morning. Throughout that night and afterwards, they remained in shock. Stephen Fairbrass, Ryan's uncle, was initially too upset to make any public comment on the matter, despite an avalanche of requests by the media. But eventually he too spoke out: 'I can't believe he could do this. He didn't seem big enough in any sense of the word to go out and do such a terrible thing. He never seemed to have the will to do anything properly. Now we must live with the shame of being connected to this man. I still can't believe that the Michael Ryan I knew is the one who gunned down these people, including his own mother. There was no doubt that Michael was spoiled, but surely this does not explain what he did. I have met many spoiled children and they don't turn into killers.'

Ryan's suicide in the John O'Gaunt School had not heralded the end of the police operation. For the emergency response now gave way to the twin roles of supporting the people of Hungerford and the huge task of investigating the incident. Over the next three weeks, more than fifty CID and other specialized officers were to be involved in bringing the investigation to a satisfactory conclusion. Enquiries were carried out to locate next of kin and witnesses. A sweep search ensured that everyone was accounted for and that no injured or dead person had been overlooked. The Casualty Bureau, opened at three o'clock that grim Wednesday afternoon, operated continuously for the following forty-eight hours, dealing with almost a thousand enquiries. A CID Major Incident Room was set up at the Thames Valley Police's Training Centre, using the Auto-Index computerized crime investigation system. And in addition to the four vehicles of the deceased, a further eleven cars were recovered from the various scenes of crime.

'On the Sunday I met Douglas Hurd at the police station,' Ron Tarry recalls. 'He was quizzed about the gun law by the press. Because we all went along to the shell of Ryan's house and saw his gun cabinet and so on. He asked some very searching questions. I was more impressed by the Prime Minister's visit, though. In fact after her visit, one town councillor, a local Tory, asked me in for a drink. I told him how well I thought she had done. This chap said that this was what he had been telling me for years, and that he would go off straight away to get me an application form to join the Conservative Party. We often used to kid one another, so I replied: "No thank you — she wasn't that bloody good." '

Sue Broughton, then the assistant senior librarian at Newbury and community librarian at Hungerford, realized early on that the town's library, situated just off the High Street, could have an important role to play in the immediate aftermath of the tragedy. Acting on her own initiative, she assembled a unique body of material, turning the small library there into a comprehensive information centre. All of her documents had at least one theme in common: how to help people rebuild their lives after the tragedy. It was a facility which was to prove extremely effective during the next few months, widely used and appreciated as it was by the people of Hungerford, and for which she would later be honoured.

Ernie Peacock, chairman of the Hungerford Town

Band, wondered whether the fête and dog show planned for the Sunday after the massacre and originally intended to raise money for the band, should be cancelled. After consulting widely, he finally decided that it should go ahead, but that all the proceeds should go instead to the Tragedy Fund. That Sunday there was an atmosphere of mourning in the air. On the fairground on Hungerford Common the Union Jack hung at half-mast on a short pole hammered in earlier that morning. Band members stood to attention dressed in black, and the proceedings began with prayers and hymns. Ron Tarry, always on hand, spoke of how the people of Hungerford were weeping, some of them silently perhaps, but weeping nonetheless.

By the end of the day Jean Strong, on the cake stall, had made £70, selling home-made scones and walnut cakes and bunches of onions from people's gardens. Her customers insisted on her keeping the change. On another table, among the mugs and saucers, were laid two toy pistols with a picture of a running commando behind them, and priced at £1.50. By the end of the afternoon's rather strained proceedings, they had still to find a buyer.

In the week following the tragedy, the epicentre of the stress it had caused was inevitably the market town itself. But many other people, many from out of town, had been affected too. Indeed a good number of the police officers who had had indirect responsibility in the earlier stages of the massacre were

themselves soon reporting many of the symptoms of
stress. The Thames Valley Police acted speedily to
make stress counselling available, through the offices
of the Force's Welfare Officers, in addition to liaising
with a trained counsellor and a consultant psychiatrist.

Still riding on a tidal wave of spiritual support and
Christian love, the Reverend Salt continued to
administer his own brand of counselling. 'I don't know
what we really mean by bereavement,' he would later
reflect. 'Maybe we are talking about trying to release
pain. But I think, initially, for many people, it may
just come out as physical pain. Just as, if I was to jump
on someone's foot, they might howl. And there was
indeed this immediate, physical reaction. Then there's
also the mental pain — the kind of thing you get
when a small child hurts itself but doesn't actually cry
until it catches up with mummy. And then, of course,
there can be a kind of spiritual pain in trying to
reconcile and get meaning from all of that.'

Ron Tarry was experiencing every one of these
pains. But he could find no meaning in anything that
Ryan had done. He decided, however, unconsciously
perhaps, that to a certain extent his own grief and
questioning would have to be deferred, for there was
simply too much work to be done. During the first
week after the tragedy Mayor Tarry was seldom out of
camera shot. There were times, during those first few
days, when representatives of the media would be
queuing at his doorstep in Sarum Way.

'I thought that this was a role I could usefully

carry out. In fact when I announced the creation of the Tragedy Fund, on the balcony of the town hall, there were hundreds upon hundreds of press there. I am amazed to this day that I wasn't absolutely panic-stricken. But you gain the strength from somewhere. I knew what I wanted to say. It was a challenge. I thought I could do it. That I had to do it. And that it had to be me. So, again, I would say to myself, "Just be yourself. Don't put on any airs. Just be yourself."'

When the broadcaster and journalist Sandy Gall had read the news on ITN's *News at Ten* that Wednesday evening, he had begun thus: 'Hungerford before today was known as a peaceful town.' He could hardly have put it more succinctly, for as the modest Mayor went on to explain on that same news bulletin: 'This town will never be the same again.'

14.
'Jesus Christ Bless you, Hannah'

As the Hungerford Family Help Unit began to establish itself, and cash and cheques continued to arrive at the town hall, so the funeral parlours of Berkshire suddenly found themselves with business they would rather not have had. For despite the previous week's surge of activity, ranging from the visit of the Prime Minister to the rather sorrowful staging of the local fête and dog show, not a single burial or cremation had taken place. Sixteen funerals were thus awaited.

PC Roger Brereton's funeral was scheduled to take place on Thursday, 27 August. But Liz Brereton was to see her husband before that: 'I asked to be taken to see him at a chapel of rest. He was lying there looking like he did when I first met him. He looked so young. I could tell by the look on his face that he hadn't died in agony. I remember making some stupid remark like: "Doesn't he look well!" And then I told him that I loved him very much.'

It was their last private moment together, for Roger Brereton's funeral was very much a public affair. Over 400 people attended, including 250 police officers representing most of Britain's forty-three forces. Douglas Hurd was present for the service at the parish church of St Mary's in Shaw-cum-Donnington, on the outskirts of Newbury. The Metropolitan Police Commissioner, Mr, later Sir, Peter Imbert, attended too. Seven uniformed police motorcyclists led the funeral cortège, with a twenty-six-strong police guard of honour lining the path to the tiny sandstone church. Six officers carried the coffin, draped in the Thames Valley Police flag, whose Latin motto translates as 'Let There be Peace in Thames Valley', and upon which PC Brereton's cap had been placed. Softly, the organist played 'The Lord is my Shepherd'. The Chief Constable of the Thames Valley Police, Colin Smith, paid tribute to his constable: 'It is so tragic, but perhaps appropriate if his life had to be so cruelly cut short, that he should die when, aware of the risks, he went right into the centre of a very dangerous situation with the clear intention of trying to help save the lives of the people of Hungerford.'

As the service continued, Liz Brereton looked around the packed church. All around her tears were being shed. Her two teenaged sons, relatives, friends, policemen, policewomen, officials of all kinds: they were all unable or unwilling to restrain their grief. Not Liz Brereton, though: 'I wanted to cry. But I just couldn't. All I experienced was just a few tears when they handed me his cap after the cremation. But that was all.'

The Reverend Salt was wrestling with a dilemma of an altogether more practical nature. It was clear that, with Hungerford continuing to be the focus of worldwide media attention, especially now that the funerals were taking place, his words to the bereaved would receive widespread publicity. And it was equally clear that many VIPs were going to attend. Nor had the vicar ever officiated at the joint burial of a husband and wife, a fate that now awaited Myrtle and Jack Gibbs, into whose house Ryan had stormed. He was to succeed, however, in finding the additional strength necessary to carry him through those early, traumatic days. While it was unthinkable to simply repeat the same sermon for each funeral, the Reverend Salt was nonetheless able to identify a common theme. This was that what mattered most was the knowledge that in terms of death people are not divided, either with God or, in Hungerford's current situation, as a community.

Funerals and fund-raising went on simultaneously. Plans were soon in hand for a wide variety of events.

One Bloody Afternoon

An all-star rugby match was arranged in support of the appeal, and a celebrity cricket match. As a housebound pensioner was offering to make soft toys to sell, with the proceeds going to the fund, organizers from the Welsh male-voice choirs of Llanelli and Cwmbach gathered to see how they too might be able to help. Amounts ranging from as little as 2p, from children's pocket money, to cheques for up to £10,000 continued to find their way to the fund. A member of the Rootes family contributed £5,000, and a local garage donated a Nissan car worth the same amount.

Celebrities from the world of entertainment discussed the making of a record, the royalties from which would go to the appeal. The pop singer Sinitta, the *Coronation Street* star Chris Quentin, the *EastEnders* actor Leonard Fenton and the singer Marti Webb liaised via their agents to see if they might not be able to collaborate on a project. Meanwhile, a sponsored cycle ride was being organized, in addition to a mass display by the Kent Parascending Team. Even a local thief appeared to have been overcome by an outbreak of conscience. Having stolen the contents of a collection box for the fund from the Halfway House pub in nearby Kintbury, he telephoned the pub's manager to inform him that not only would he be returning the cash, albeit anonymously, he would also be adding a contribution of his own.

That telephone call was made on Friday, 28 August, the same day as the funeral of Sue Godfrey,

Ryan's first victim. She was buried at the parish church of St Mary the Virgin in her home village of Burghfield Common. More than fifty wreaths were laid in the churchyard, and over two hundred mourners were present, including the two Wiltshire police officers who had found Sue's body, riddled with bullets, in the Savernake Forest eleven days earlier. Hannah and James Godfrey heard the Reverend David Smith speak of their mother's great kindness. Both were clutching cuddly toys, as if, one newspaper put it the following day, 'teddy eases the pain'.

The vicar asked a question to which he was unable to provide even the hint of an answer: 'Why did it have to happen, especially to someone so gentle, so loving, so caring, so much involved in the community in which she lived a life spent caring for others? Someone described her as a small person in a big uniform with a big heart and an even bigger smile. She was always bubbling over, she was always smiling, and even the most sick and pain-stricken patients had a different glow come over them when she was in their presence. With her sudden and tragic passing we know it can never be the same again. An area of life, a familiar voice, a known footstep has sadly disappeared and cannot ever be re-created.'

Unaware of why she and her brother were the centre of attention, Hannah clung tightly to an aunt with one hand and to a rag doll with the other. Her pink dress and yellow ribbons echoed the flowers that were strewn beside the path to her mother's grave. It was not Hannah's first visit to the church in recent days, for she had attended the latter part of a service the previous Sunday, immediately after religious classes that day. Then, the Reverend Jeffrey Daley, kneeling before the altar, had laid his hands on the little girl's blonde hair and uttered the words: 'Jesus Christ bless you, Hannah, whereupon almost the entire congregation had broken down with the raw agony of grief.

Five days after their mother had been laid to rest, the children left a wreath of roses and carnations by her grave. Their message was simple, and written in childish scrawl: 'To Mummy — all our love.' Next to it lay a wreath from their father, Brian Godfrey, 'Wish you were here, Sue — all my love', it read.

Mayor Tarry, as busy as ever, was suffering too: 'The awfulness of the tragedy was driven home to me at the funerals. I went to seven or eight of them within two days. They are bad enough at the best of times. But it was the repeating and the repeating of the funerals. Sandra Hill used to live just around the corner from me, and I knew her father quite well. I went to her cremation at Oxford. She had just come back to Hungerford to see some friends. She was young. The chapel was full of young people. That was the last funeral I went to. I couldn't speak to the parents afterwards. I was just exhausted. She had just chanced to be in Hungerford that day. I was very upset indeed then. I thought, I can't take much more of this. That really was a low point for me. But there was so much else to do, I simply had to get on.'

The first of the funerals had taken place two days earlier, on Wednesday, 26 August, exactly one week after the massacre. It was the funeral of Eric Vardy. At the graveside, his widow, Marlyne, wept uncontrollably. Clutching a spray of red roses, she heard the Reverend Nigel Sands speak eloquently about a shocked and stunned rural community. Addressing the mourners in the twelfth-century parish church of St Mary's in Great Shefford, West Berkshire, he said: 'We have from afar become blasé about news of violence and sudden death in Ireland and the Middle East. But when it came to our doorsteps or, for one family, into our living-room, we learned in the most awful manner that murder and mayhem are not confined to Beirut and Belfast.'

In fact another irony haunted the death of Eric Vardy. For one year earlier, Marlyne and Eric Vardy had together made arrangements for her funeral rather than his. This was because medical experts had deemed it extremely unlikely that Marlyne, although only in her forties, would survive major cancer surgery. But she had defied their judgement, and thus it fell to her, not Eric, to write the wording of a wreath. She chose a heart of red roses on a bed of white carnations, the flowers bearing her final message of farewell:

Time cannot dim the face I love,

One Bloody Afternoon

The memory of your smile,
The countless things you did for me
To make my life worthwhile.
You've left a place no one can fill
In my heart you'll live forever

Love, Marlyne

Day after day, it seemed, in every corner of Berkshire, funerals were taking place. More than 200 people attended the funeral of Mr Abdul Rahman Khan, as Muslim mourners paid their last respects. Chief Constable Colin Smith led a contingent of Thames Valley police officers at the cremation of Douglas Wainwright, shot down in his car. His widow, Kathleen, herself injured in the shooting, attended the service wearing a sling. And as that cremation was taking place, more than 300 people crowded into St Lawrence's, to hear the Reverend Salt conduct the double funeral of Myrtle and Jack Gibbs, in the presence of their four sons and three daughters. As he did so, less than half a mile away a private family service was being held for Francis Butler, the twenty-six-year-old accounts clerk gunned down while walking his dog.

The funeral service of Dorothy Ryan, the gunman's mother, was one of the few to face rows of empty pews. Some forty mourners attended the service, which was conducted by Canon John Reynolds. He chose to avoid any mention of her son and made only the most fleeting of references to the massacre he had perpetrated at Hungerford. Although the Canon described Mrs Ryan as a kind, warm and generous person, he made no mention of her role as a devoted mother to the man who, ten days earlier, had shot her dead as she begged for her life to be spared. The funeral was held at St Mary's Church in Calne, Wiltshire, Dorothy Ryan's birthplace and the home of her sister, Mrs Nora Fairbrass. A senior officer from the Thames Valley Police attended the funeral, as did a representative of Hungerford Town Council. Nobody doubted that Dorothy Ryan was herself a victim, and indeed her grave was heaped with flowers, including an anonymous circle of white chrysanthemums with the message: 'With Christian Love — From One Mother to Another.'

Another mother in some difficulty during that week of funerals was Jenny Barnard. The cremation of her husband, Barney, took place on the same day as Roger Brereton's, and it was the first of the funerals to be held in the massacre town itself. More than 300 people attended the service conducted by the Reverend Wallace Edwards in the town's Methodist chapel. As Jenny Barnard held their silently sleeping five-week-old son Joe tightly to her chest, 'Bridge over Troubled Waters', Barney's favourite tune, was played as the cabby's coffin was carried in.

'He was a bridge over troubled waters to many people,' said the Methodist minister. 'One of the characters who made Hungerford tick. Barney had such plans for Joe. He is the son Barney adored. We are grateful that he had him, if only for five weeks. This little boy represents an opportunity to us all. We cannot undo what happened last week, but we can help Jenny, Joe's mother, to bring him up as Barney would have wanted her to do.'

As Wallace Edwards read from the Book of Lamentations and the Gospel of St John, Jenny Barnard, dressed in black, sobbed and shook uncontrollably. 'Barney brought sunshine into old people's lives,' the minister said. 'Sometimes he didn't even collect his fares. He cared for people and carried them. God worked through Barney and this was his way of answering our prayers. Of course the effect of this tragedy will stay with us for a long time. We are a tight-knit community. But I do see a little light at the end of the tunnel. He is a little light shining in our darkness. And his name is Joe.'

Not so very far away, at Newbury Baptist Church, the Reverend Granville Overton was officiating at the burial service of Ian Playle, the Justices' clerk. He had died in hospital some forty-eight hours after being shot by Ryan. His widow immediately agreed that his heart and kidneys could be used for transplantation. By doing this and helping others, the minister said, Ian Playle's love of life was being perpetuated. And so, all around Hungerford, the funerals were to continue. One after another, throughout that week, until Roland and Sheila Mason, Ken Clements and George White — and eventually all sixteen of Ryan's victims had likewise been laid to rest. 'Social services asked me if I was all right,' recalls Ron Tarry. 'They asked how I was coping. My wife told them that this is how he spends his life — rushing around — so let him rush around now — it's what he knows best. But the next week I spent just exhausted and flat. But all the time the functions were going on. As Mayor I had to go along to receive the money, so that sort of carried me through. Groups of children would have large sales, often selling off their own toys. One sale raised £12. That touched me as much as the larger donations. Others had had a sponsored silence. And I remember thinking at the time how delighted the parents must have been to see their children raise money in that way.'

David Lee, the headmaster of the John O'Gaunt School, was in something of a quandary. Ryan had taken refuge in the school after the shootings. There, he had made his way into Room 6, used mainly for English lessons, where he had himself been taught. Having barricaded the door with a filing cabinet, table and chairs, he had conducted a tense conversation with Sergeant Brightwell from that room. And it was there, too, that he had taken his own life. Days later Ryan's blood was still on the walls; the windows remained smashed. But exercising the mind of the headmaster was the fact that exactly twenty days after the massacre, some 700 children were due to begin the new school year.

David Lee wondered what his approach should be.

'I dread to think what would have happened if all of this had taken place when the school had been occupied,' he admitted. 'The town has had a traumatic experience, and so have the children. But it's not for me to protect them from reality. I think to pretend that nothing had happened would be ridiculous.'

By the time the pupils returned on Tuesday, 8 September they found the room in which Ryan had taken refuge looking spick and span. It had been completely redecorated and refurbished, and all traces of the recent events eliminated. Nonetheless, a team of counsellors and psychiatrists stood by, ready to help any child who might be having difficulty coping with the chilling thought of being taught in a room where a former pupil had taken his own life immediately after slaughtering sixteen people. But the team of experts found themselves without work that day. David Lee had every reason to feel proud of his pupils, and he did.

Two weeks and two days after the start of the school term, the spotlight was once again on Hungerford, for the inquest was about to begin. The coroner for West Berkshire, Charles Hoile, instructed the jury that it was up to them to examine the fury and ferocity of Ryan's attack. Jurors were handed booklets containing photographs of the bodies and the area where the victims had met their deaths. Piled under a pink blanket were Ryan's two semi-automatic rifles and the Beretta pistol with which he had taken his own life. His bloodstained body armour and battledress jacket were also waiting to be displayed. Evidence was taken from Thomas Warlow, a firearms expert. Then Dr Richard Shepherd, a forensic pathologist, gave graphic and detailed accounts of the wounds and probable causes of death of each of the victims.

Altogether, seventy-three statements were selected for use in court. Some were to be delivered in person by the witness, in which case further questioning could take place, while others, like Hannah Godfrey's, were simply read. Throughout the four-day hearing, nuns from a Franciscan community in the area took responsibility for welcoming and caring for people who came or who were brought to them in the hall. The Hungerford Family Help Unit was again in action, working closely with the Registrar of Births, Marriages and Deaths in the task of collecting death certificates after the hearing. Unit staff were also involved throughout the hearings providing support for witnesses and relatives alike. The inquest was undoubtedly another milestone in the events set in train by that fateful Wednesday afternoon. So much had happened in Hungerford, and yet the massacre had taken place just one month earlier.

Liz Brereton was continuing to receive a great deal of support from both family and friends. But she kept insisting that she simply did not need any of the professional help which was constantly being offered to her. 'That's the trouble with me,' she would later admit, 'I'm terribly stubborn. I did have some support, but not full-scale counselling. It was only when my dog had to be put down, a little later on, that it all came out. Ben was my husband Roger's dog, a border collie, but he was my shadow. When I heard the news, I just dropped the phone, and that was it, it all came out that day. Then I just couldn't stop. This trigger of the dog was like coming out of a cage for me, because it was only then that I really began to realize precisely what I had lost. Not just my partner and friend, but a future too. Then, the tears really did come in earnest, and they still do. And I suppose that has to be a good thing.'

Because the shooting of Sue Godfrey had taken place in Wiltshire rather than Berkshire, a separate inquest had to be held. Once again the experts were out, relaying the minutiae of her death as part of the official procedures which had to be followed. During the first few weeks after the murder of their mother both Hannah and James repeatedly wet their beds. Neither of them could sleep and kept making their way to their father's bedroom. From the outset, though, Brian Godfrey's courage had shone through. 'No matter how bleak things look now,' he insisted at the time, 'I am determined to hold things together for the sake of the children. But God knows what they must be going through.'

With all the innocence of their age, Hannah and James would speak of the nasty man who took Mummy away and shot her. With the blunt honesty of small children, they would talk openly about the killing. It was only when they would fall or hurt themselves that they would cry out for the mother they had lost. Brian Godfrey reveals: 'They talk about it quite frequently. They are very frank about it. In fact it's sometimes difficult to cope with the way they are talking about it. It takes people by surprise. Shortly before the inquest James fell over and hurt himself. He was crying out, asking for Mummy. We had a big crying session and I told them that Mummy would not be coming back. Hannah has been particularly protective towards her brother. As for me, I seemed to have a constant headache for weeks on end, though. I just felt sick. In those early days I would go into each of the children's rooms, before they went to sleep each night and say: "Right, any worries, questions, problems." I remember that James was very sweet one night. I walked in and before I could speak he said: "I not got no problems, Daddy." I thought, well, at least one of us is doing all right.'

On Thursday, 8 October 1987 a memorial and rededication service was held for the town of Hungerford. It was, according to Mayor Tarry, the day on which life in the town could begin again. Three thousand grieving townsfolk, some sixty per cent of the population of Hungerford, huddled against the cold by the steps of the town hall in a moving open-air service, shared with millions of television viewers. Once again, the flag on the town hall fluttered at half-mast. The Reverend Salt, who was responsible for much of the organization, bid everyone welcome that evening, and said: 'Together we now place ourselves before Almighty God, our Heavenly Father. May we, who have been preserved, dedicate ourselves anew to His service. May we offer ourselves to each other in the life of our community, with respect for every human soul, and with thankfulness for all God's gifts to us. To Almighty God, our Creator, and the defender of every soul, living and departed, be all praise and glory, now and for ever. Amen.'

It was the closest anybody was to get, that evening, to mentioning the name of Michael Ryan. As the list of the deceased was read out by Mayor Tarry, the gunman's name, a hard one to utter in that grieving town, was deliberately omitted.

The VIPs were out in force. The Queen and Prince Philip were represented by the Lord Lieutenant of Berkshire, Colonel the Hon. Gordon Palmer. The junior Home Office minister, Douglas Hogg, stood in for the Prime Minister. The Prince and Princess of Wales were represented by Prince Harry's godfather, the Hon. Gerald Ward, a wealthy West Berkshire landowner and one of the three trustees of the Tragedy Fund.

The principal sermon was preached by the Archbishop of Canterbury, the most Reverend and Right Honourable Robert Runcie. He was convinced that Hungerford was already on the road to recovery, as he said: 'The sharing of hurt is often the beginning of its healing. And all that I have heard about the people of this town and your reaction to this tragedy convinces me that the healing process has already begun. Those of you there that day shared in common fear and bewilderment. It was then that you became companions in adversity. And such companionship in adversity has its own good and healing power. It breeds not bitterness but warmth. You have already begun to build your life on the stories you have to tell. I think of Susan Godfrey, the first victim, whose calm and measured response saved the lives of her children. They will grow knowing her story and so learning how closely love and sacrifice are linked. I think too of Police Constable Roger Brereton, whose courage cost him his life, who knew that the community looked to him for its own safety.'

Just before the Archbishop's address, there was a commemoration of the departed. It came in the form of a poem written by the Reverend Geoffrey Carr, formerly Rural Dean of Bradfield:

Deep Sympathy to Hungerford, August 1987

History has been kind the centuries down
To our beloved, ancient, quiet town;
Many have lived and died in peace while bearing
Our mede of human ills and pain and sharing,
Until the holocaust of a bright summer's day
Swept, in the crash of shots, our peace away.

One Bloody Afternoon

Before, no thought could ever have conceived
Such bloody ending to the way we lived;
Before we took for granted we lived far
From crimes of madness, so much worse than war.
We still cannot believe a Godhating devil
Could turn a neighbour's mind to speechless evil.

But 2000 years ago, to kill a child
A king by fear and jealousy made wild,
Deliberately, knocking door to door
Sent soldiers; no regard for rich or poor,
To snatch each baby boy, two years and under,

From family and life to rend asunder.
No words can fully tell our grief or theirs,
But weeping we can turn to One Who cares.
Mary was saved from Bethlehem mother's loss
Only to watch her Son upon the Cross …

He broke the awful power of crime and death;
Tortured, yet praying with each pain-filled breath
'Father, forgive, they know not what they do'
He lives to heal and love and comfort you.

He promises the world the Day will come
When tears, pain, death will no more rend a home.
Men will learn war no more, a child shall lead
The lion; savage beasts together feed.
So hope, bearing this bitter cross, be blest,
By Jesus . . . 'Come, and I will give you rest.'

'Jesus Christ Bless You, Hannah'

The people of Hungerford had assembled in the open air because an abbey or cathedral would have been too small a venue for such a multitude, and too remote from the town. Nonetheless, to assemble on the steps of the town hall was an odd, risky choice. In fact it was a triumph, a moving, restrained and dignified occasion; so successful indeed that many people in the town wondered if it ought not to represent the end of Hungerford's formal mourning period. Was it perhaps not the appropriate time, they asked, for the work of the Family Help Unit to cease, and thus for many of the experts from outside to now be given their marching orders?

'Of course that didn't mean that the mourning was over,' the Reverend Salt explains. 'But it was something of the turning over of a new leaf. The service gave us a definite focus. We are really called parsons — which comes from the word "persona" — the face of the community. And that was my job really, to make the community accept the situation. Because if you don't it just won't ever be possible to grow or move forwards.'

As the Tragedy Fund edged towards the £1 million mark, the composer Andrew Lloyd Webber organized a gala evening at St Nicholas's Church, Newbury, not far from his home. Sarah Brightman took the leading role in her then husband's Requiem Mass. Julian Lloyd Webber also took part, playing his cello. It was the biggest single money-raising event, providing over £50,000 for the fund. At the beginning of December, however, Ron Tarry announced that the fund was to close shortly after Christmas. In the end, over £1 million was raised.

As the months passed by, the Hungerford massacre began to fade from the public's mind. This was precisely what many of the town's residents had been hoping for for some time, as the prevalent feeling now was that of wanting to be left alone. Even so, services and ceremonies continued to take place. In February 1988 the Reverend Salt participated, together with his Bishop, in a ceremony for the dedication of a memorial plaque at Hungerford. The memorial itself formed part of a screen surrounding the church's new vestry. And then, four months later, Downing Street issued an operational note announcing the Queen's civil gallantry awards. The time had come to honour some of the many heroes of Hungerford.

A letter from the Central Chancery of The Orders of Knighthood, St James's Palace, London, dated 8 June 1988, announced:

The Queen has been graciously pleased to approve the award of the Queen's Commendation for Brave Conduct to the undermentioned:

Roger Brereton (deceased), Lately Constable, Thames Valley Police

Linda Constance, Mrs Bright, Ambulancewoman, Berkshire Ambulance Service

Miss Carol Irene Hall, Air Stewardess, British

Airways plc

Carl Peter Lawrence Harries, Lance Corporal,
The Royal Engineers

Hazel Jacqueline, Mrs Haslett, Ambulancewoman,
Berkshire Ambulance Service

Michael Thomas Palmer, Supervisor, Newbury
District Council

David John Sparrow, Lifeguard and Attendant,
Newbury District Council

Jeremy John Wood, Constable, Thames Valley
Police

In recognition of bravery following the shooting
incident at Hungerford, Berkshire, on 19th August
1987.

The gallantry awards were presented by Prince
Charles a few weeks later at a ceremony at County
Hall in Oxford, at which the Prince spoke to the
recipients and their families. Liz Brereton attended,
together with her two sons, Shaun and Paul. Holding
the award certificate and two silver laurel leaves, she
made the briefest of statements to the assembled press
corps: 'All I want to say is that I am very, very proud.'
Did this indicate, perhaps, that eleven months after
the massacre, Liz Brereton was beginning to emerge
from her period of mourning? It did not.

'Actually I used to spend quite a lot of time
thinking about suicide,' Liz recalls. 'Because I was so
desperate to be with Roger again. I was thinking of

any possible way of joining him. But I knew that deep down I wouldn't really have done it. What would have happened to my sons — and what about the grief I would then have inflicted upon my own parents and in-laws? Still, the first Christmas without Roger was pretty terrible. I came into the kitchen and the boys came in after me and we had a good cry together.'

On 28 July 1988 a Garden Party took place at Buckingham Palace. Both Ron Tarry and the Reverend David Salt received an invitation to attend. 'Maybe that was a reward, I don't know,' Ron Tarry would later reflect. 'My wife and I, and our younger daughter, Claire, were presented to the Queen on that occasion. We went along with the Salts. A few days before it was due to take place the Lord Chamberlain's office rang to say that Her Majesty would like to meet me. I obviously couldn't go in my old Escort, so the local garage lent me a Granada, because we had been given VIP parking in the grounds of the Palace. I found the Queen to be very informed. It was comparatively relaxed. As I was talking, I was trying to concentrate, of course, but also to savour the moment. That here I am on the Palace lawn, me, Ron Tarry from nowhere, talking to the Queen.'

If the people of Hungerford thought that now that almost one year had passed since the tragedy, they would be left alone, they were mistaken. On the contrary, as the first anniversary of the massacre approached, it was for the media yet another opportunity to revisit the town. On Sunday, 14 August 1988, just five days before the first anniversary, the BBC screened a documentary in the *Everyman* series, charting the plight of the grieving town. Fortunately it was a sensitive, reflective piece of television journalism. In her contribution to the programme Jenny Barnard developed the theme of the changing nature of grief. 'Well, I've now come to realize that there is a meaning to my life. And the meaning of my life is Joe. He makes life worth living. I have now started to feel that life is worth living. I used to feel guilty about actually going out and laughing. But I've got over that stage now. I know that Barney would have wanted me to have gone out and laughed and joked. But as for that awful cliché "light at the end of the tunnel", well, I can see that there is probably light at the end of the tunnel. But how far along the tunnel I am I really couldn't say. Because some days you seem as though you're way up. And on another day you're back down again.'

Writing in the *Newbury Weekly News*, Ron Tarry issued a plea for self-restraint by the press: 'As we approach the anniversary of that dreadful day last year, I am sure that I am echoing the feelings of many people in Hungerford who feel that, if television, radio and the national press must mention the date, they do so reverently and without sensationalizing the event.'

It was a plea which fell on deaf ears in some quarters of the press. In fact many of the townspeople went away for the day when 19 August finally arrived. All of the town's shops closed. But wreaths placed at the Hungerford war memorial amply demonstrated that the guilt peculiar to survivors had still to be eradicated in the town. 'Sorry I could not save you,' one card read, 'but I tried to do so. I will never forget.'

Liz Brereton also had reason to reflect on that sad day: 'Well, as for the posthumous medal and all that, I say: "Look what I had to lose to get this." They all told me that Roger died a hero. I didn't want him to be a hero. I just wanted him to be alive.'

15.
'If Only We Knew Why'

The first anniversary of the tragedy at Hungerford was an opportunity for many in the media, not just to reconstruct the minutiae of the massacre but also to examine afresh Michael Ryan's motives. No answers had been provided in the immediate aftermath of the tragedy; perhaps they would be forthcoming some twelve months later. Many newspapers and television companies, both national and local, sent reporters and producers back to the town in the hope of achieving some new insight. In fact nothing new was uncovered.

Thus it was that, despite diligently carrying out his duties, a reporter on the *Bolton Evening News* was able only to echo the theme of enduring incomprehensibility. It was a theme which was to appear in a good many of those anniversary articles. 'Twelve months of soul-searching have passed, but one question remains unanswered,' the reporter affirmed. 'Why, in God's name, did it happen?'

'It's actually very frustrating to be asked that question,' the Reverend Salt is now quick to retort. 'The how, why and wherefore and so on. No one has ever explained why Michael Ryan did what he did. And that's because, in my opinion, it is not something that can be explained.'

But in an age where instant answers are available for all things, the vicar's view has not been easy to accept. Surely, people continue to insist, there has to be a compelling explanation. For many, the first line of enquiry leads them to a person who exists only on celluloid. For were not the exploits of the character Rambo in the film *First Blood* so strikingly similar to what actually took place in Hungerford as to be uncanny? Indeed, the *Sunday Telegraph* was soon asking, was Michael Ryan not 'the man who thought he was Rambo'? London's *Evening Standard* saw things slightly differently, more in terms of his aspirations. No, Ryan was 'the lonely wimp who wanted to be Rambo'.

The Rambo factor certainly made good copy. In fact there was a stage when tabloid editors were vigorously competing to print the most Ramboesque headline. For within twenty-four hours of the tragedy, the *Sun* referred no longer to Hungerford but 'the Rambo shootings'. The *Daily Mirror* followed suit by insisting that the sixteen deaths were the result of 'the Rambo killings'. Both papers then proceeded to pepper their pages with sketches of semi-automatic weaponry, just in case any reader might have failed to make the Rambo connection. The *Daily Star* was less subtle still, covering its front page with just two things: a large picture of Michael Ryan and the word RAMBO emblazoned beneath in bold type. The popular press, then, was in no doubt: Ryan and Rambo were synonymous. Michael Ryan was John Rambo.

The truth was a lot less colourful. For it is simply not known whether or not Ryan ever saw any of Sylvester Stallone's films, including *First Blood*. Furthermore, academic research has yet to prove conclusively that there is a causal link between screen violence and real-life aggression. In their search for instant solutions to complex problems, many people, often with the encouragement of the media, were apparently too ready to jump to ill-conceived conclusions. It had been the same story in the previous decade, when the film *A Clockwork Orange* appeared. Then, researchers cited the murder of a tramp in what appeared to be a copycat crime. The incident was soon dubbed the '*Clockwork Orange* murder' by the popular press, but the study omitted to point out one important fact: that the tramp's killer had never seen the film supposed to have incited him to murder.

It came as no surprise, however, to find Sylvester Stallone leaping to the defence of his screen persona. He preferred to dwell on the concept of insanity rather than imitation. And in so doing he would not be alone. 'I carry the can for every lunatic in the world who goes crazy with a gun,' he complained. 'But it wasn't Rambo who sent Michael Ryan mad. In fact Rambo is the opposite of people like Ryan. He is always up against stronger opposition and never shoots first. Murderers are always saying, "God told me to kill" or "Jesus ordered me to kill" — so should the rest of us stop praying? There are always sick people out there who will hang their illness on to your hook.'

For those newspapers and magazines less willing to go down the Rambo road there remained little else to proffer by way of explanation. Their watchwords were invariably the same: Ryan's rampage was 'meaningless', 'random' or 'motiveless'. Then more reflective pieces began to appear, dwelling on the precise nature of the 'loner'. For no one doubted that Ryan was that. 'Beware the man who walks alone,' warned one paper, while another referred to 'the maniac next door'.

However, it was not just readers of the tabloids who sought an explanation of Ryan's motives. Many people in Hungerford, survivors included, did so too. Alison Chapman, herself shot at as she set out from her home with her mother, comments: 'If only he had lived long enough to tell us why. If only we knew why. But instead he took the secret of his madness to his grave.'

The Archbishop of Canterbury appeared to endorse this notion of Ryan's insanity, in his sermon preached at the town's service of memorial and rededication. 'Sometimes violence can be understood,' he admitted. 'Oppressed peoples rising against their oppressors or the grossly deprived revolting against unheeding opulence — these things might be foreseen or forestalled. But no one could foresee this tragedy. The human mind is the most complex and delicately balanced of all created things. Wisdom cannot foresee all the consequences of its sickness.'

Were signs of a consensus beginning to emerge? If Ryan was not the Rambo figure the tabloids might have wished him to be, was he without doubt certifiably insane? Sylvester Stallone, although not an impartial witness, had dubbed him a lunatic; survivor Alison Chapman spoke of his madness; and then, most authoritative of all Dr Robert Runcie had described to an audience of several millions the apparent sickness of a human mind. What each person was saying, some more delicately than others, was that Michael Ryan was mad.

Dwelling on Ryan's insanity, however, is almost as problematic as attempting to package him as the Rambo-like killer. For contrary to popular opinion, there is little evidence of insanity among the majority of mass killers. In a forty-two-case sample study by the American criminologists Levin and Fox, only around one in five killers attempted to plead not guilty by reason of insanity. And of those who did, less than half would manage to convince a jury.

In their authoritative report Professors Levin and Fox went on to present a 'composite profile' of the multiple-victim killer. They came to the conclusion that the great majority of such killers were not insane; that, in layman's terms, they were bad rather than mad: 'He is typically a white male in his late twenties or thirties. In the case of simultaneous mass murder, he kills people he knows with a handgun or rifle; in serial crimes, he murders strangers by beating or strangulation. The specific motivation depends on the circumstances leading up to the crime, but it generally deals directly with either money, expediency, jealousy, or lust ... Finally, though the mass killer often may appear cold and show no remorse, and even deny responsibility for his crime, serious mental illness or psychosis is rarely present.'

The two academics were also able to identify a number of factors which, they believe, are consistent with almost every case history of an indiscriminate killer. First of all, they argue, there has been a life filled with frustration. Secondly, there has been a precipitating event, such as unemployment or divorce. Then there is access to and training in the use of firearms. And finally there has been a breakdown of what is referred to as 'social controls', such as occurs when a person moves to a new town or an important relationship breaks up.

Ryan would certainly have fitted into this model. His had been a life of frustration, as he drifted from one unskilled job to the next. And Ryan not only had access to and training in firearms, but they were the theme around which his entire life revolved, a passion which had endured for well over a decade. The problem with such a construction, however, is that large numbers of ordinary people can fall within these categories — people who do not go on to commit mass murder. While Professor Levin clearly did not have the opportunity to analyse or study Ryan's personality, he nonetheless refuses to entertain the notion of Ryan's insanity: 'I don't like the idea of insanity in these cases and it is used rarely in the US as a defence. Insanity removes the question of individual responsibility and these people are usually a lot more rational than people think.'

Certainly Sergeant Paul Brightwell would testify to that. And yet an equally impressive selection of authorities from the world of psychiatry came to precisely the opposite conclusion. The criminologists had got it the wrong way round, they would insist. Ryan was mad, not bad.

Dr John Hamilton, the medical director of Broadmoor, the Berkshire prison for the criminally insane, was of the opinion that Ryan was probably suffering from a form of schizophrenia and was certainly psychotic at the time he carried out the killings. He diagnosed Ryan's disorder as paranoid schizophrenia, adding that he was in all likelihood suffering from paranoid delusions too. Dr Jim Higgins, a consultant forensic psychiatrist for Mersey Regional Health Authority, and one of the country's leading authorities on mental illness, agreed with this diagnosis: 'Matricide is the schizophrenic crime — that is an aphorism in forensic psychiatry. Ryan was most likely to be suffering from acute schizophrenia. He might have had a reason for doing what he did, but it was likely to be bizarre and peculiar to him. But the people who are murdered are generally part of the murderer's family or social circle, so the murder of strangers is very unusual. Ryan was, in my opinion, also likely to have been suffering from ideas of persecution. People with acute schizophrenia may believe that they are being persecuted by certain people and are entitled to shoot them.'

Of course, 'mentally ill Michael' does not have the same ring about it as 'Rambo Ryan'. It is hardly surprising, therefore, that little has been said or written about the gunman's psyche. But then mental illness is always difficult to understand, and all the more daunting to contemplate in the aftermath of a massacre. Moreover, it is worth asking whether or not the psychiatrists' opinions represent the definitive view. For the truth is that there are over a quarter of a million people in Britain suffering from schizophrenia, which, in reality, is widely used as a catch-all term for many different sorts of mental disorder. And if he was indeed schizophrenic, Ryan was certainly the first, in Britain at least, to have taken it upon himself to spray bullets at each and every unfortunate soul who happened to cross his path. Such diagnoses therefore remain a matter of speculation.

What is clearer, however, is the extent to which Ryan wove a fantasy world around himself. This emerged at the inquest with great clarity as one of the prime components in his psychological make-up. One person after another related the fantastic tales he had told. These fantasies created a lifestyle which Ryan knew very well he was never going to achieve. There was the rich colonel of Cold Ash, the nurse he had planned to marry, stories of Ferraris and Porsches which were due to come his way, trips to India and visits to tea plantations there, reports of property deals in London and a planned trip on the Orient Express. Many people had believed him, including his own mother. But every detail had been furnished by his imagination; his exploits were a tissue of lies from start to finish.

The police view has long been that Ryan had planned to sexually assault Sue Godfrey, his first victim. When the young mother and nurse had realized his intentions, they think, she had tried to run away. But no one has ever succeeded in explaining why this first murder in the forest should have been a prelude to the massacre in Hungerford.

It was precisely because the truth was no longer available that the door was left open for cranks of all kinds. The *Sun* paid several thousand pounds to one Andrew Preston for what the newspaper considered to be a first-class story. Under the headline 'Maniac Rambo was my Gay Lover — Ryan's kinky secret revealed', there appeared a graphic account of homosexual activity in the Savernake Forest. This 'exclusive' was later revealed as an elaborate hoax, the result of a dare Preston had risen to while in a state of inebriation.

Despite the apparent credulity of all those to whom he told his stories, Ryan craved yet more fantasy. Imagine his delight, then, when he discovered that this was available via mail order. As if designed to cater specifically for his needs, Ryan is said to have paid £5 to become a subscriber to a bizarre postal game called 'Further into Fantasy'. It was a cruder version of the better-known 'Dungeons and Dragons', the most popular of such fantasy war games. Power is earned through the murder of enemies and monsters, with players growing in power and status as they execute various grisly assignments allocated to them.

Opting to be a high priest of an evil serpent god, and paying £1.50 for each turn, Ryan adopted the code-name Phodius Tei. In July 1987 he received a final challenge from Set, the game's serpent god, who lived on the planet Dorm: 'You have been one of my greatest Terran priests and as such are worthy of the power I offer. But Phodius, you have one last point to prove ... can you kill your fellow Terrans? I offer you one last challenge. Will you accept, Phodius, to go back to Terra and slay them, to devour their souls in the name of Set the immortal god?'

Two weeks later Ryan received what was to be his final message: 'When at last you awake you are standing in a forest, there is a throbbing in your head, a madness that is the exhilaration of the serpent god, you know what you must do, know what power is to be gained from this.'

Ryan had indeed stood in a forest. Sue Godfrey had discovered that. It is reasonable to assume too that there had also been a throbbing in Ryan's head, for he had taken two paracetamols on the morning of the massacre. In fact many of those who encountered Ryan that day would later refer to the blank expression on his face. 'Brain-dead' had been the most popular phrase of the day. And Ryan would himself tell Sergeant Brightwell that the entire day had been 'like a bad dream'. Had he not therefore been acting out, in his own way, these coded commands received through the post, unable or unwilling to distinguish between fantasy and reality?

Of course it is one possibility, but by no means the only one. And in any case no evidence was ever produced to prove conclusively that Ryan had participated in these bizarre fantasy games, despite an investigation carried out by the Thames Valley Police. It is, therefore, simply impossible to say with any certainty precisely why Ryan carried out the Hungerford massacre. Furthermore, it is highly unlikely that much more will ever be learned that will reveal his true state of mind. Because, as the *Sunday Times* so aptly put it: 'his last shot blew the truth away'.

As the Reverend Salt went through the hundreds of letters which were arriving each day at St Lawrence's, he found among the cash and cheques destined for the fund another poem, sent in anonymously by a member of the public. It bore no title, and was instead simply prefaced: 'Written following the sad events which occurred at Hungerford, Berkshire on August 19th 1987.' The poem reads as follows:

That peaceful summer afternoon
Old England faced a cruel reality —
When in a forest's leafy glade
One instant doubly robbed two babes
Of innocence and a mother's love.
But that was just the start …
Before the sun set that day
Many a Hungerford home
Suffered a dreadful loss,
And none knew why.
The Nation's heart missed a beat

'If Only We Knew Why'

In disbelief ...
In flooded indignation, anger;
Followed by bewilderment and shock
Soon replaced by compassion, love
For those so cruelly bereaved,
Robbed of a loved one —
None knew why.

16.
'A Basic Failure
of the Police'

'Some people have said the police didn't do a good job,' Ron Tarry recalls indignantly. 'I don't agree with that at all. I thought that they did and I said so at the time to the Home Secretary. It's just all too easy to blame the police. It's true that there was quite a long delay in getting armed police into Hungerford. But people have to remember that the arms they were able to call upon locally were no match for a Kalashnikov semi-automatic rifle. And on top of that the Thames Valley hit squad happened to be situated quite some distance away.'

But this is not to imply, Ron Tarry is equally quick to point out, that nothing could have been improved in terms of policing and that mistakes were not made. Such an approach was itself mistaken and far too complacent. Of course there were lessons to be learned. 'But in the end you can only blame Michael Ryan,' the former Mayor concludes. 'Because he had the weapons, the ammunition and the will to use them.'

It was a typically balanced appraisal from Ron Tarry. Nonetheless, there were a number of people who indeed sought to blame not Michael Ryan but the officers of the Thames Valley Police. If they could not have prevented the incident happening, it was argued, then they should at the very least have brought the shootings to a much more speedy conclusion.

In fact it was not just those people who might have had a vested interest in attacking the police who became most vociferous in their criticism of the armed response to Hungerford. Colin Greenwood, a former Superintendent and firearms instructor in the West Yorkshire Police, repeatedly made a number of scathing remarks. Nor was he prepared to quietly document his criticisms in the form of a confidential memorandum to Charles Pollard, the Assistant Chief Constable of the Thames Valley Police. For the retired policeman, who had gone on to become the editor of the magazine *Guns Review*, decided instead to go public, voicing his opinions to millions of television viewers. Appearing on a special Thames Television programme, broadcast some six months after the massacre and entitled *Hungerford — the lessons*, he was presented as the key and most authoritative witness prepared to articulate the case against the inadequacy of the police response.

Greenwood did not mince his words: 'The basic fact is that Ryan went on killing people as long as he wanted, and the police didn't stop him. At no time did the police do anything to stop Ryan shooting people. That's a basic failure of the police. At no stage did the armed police confront Ryan. We know that the Tactical Unit [Firearms Team] was kept as a unit because it is said they operate as a team, which is really quite nonsensical. We know that the local police were assembled on the Common and at no time did any of them confront Ryan. He stopped because he got fed up with it. What you have to ask is whether this situation was dealt with properly. And if sixteen people were killed it wasn't.'

At the heart of such criticisms lies the precise timetable of events on Wednesday, 19 August 1987. What is accepted by all parties is that the first 999 call was made at 12.40pm after a motorcyclist had witnessed the attempted murder of Kakoub Dean at the Golden Arrow Service Station at Froxfield on the A4. Nonetheless, Ryan had managed to remain on the loose for more than an hour, killing his last victim at 1.50pm. But it was not until half an hour after that, at 2.20pm, that the Tactical Firearms Team was assembled and ready to go into action. The main reason for this delay was that the only available officers from the Team that day were some forty miles away, engaged in training exercises at the Otmoor army firing range. The consequence of this was that there was in effect no tactical firearms cover in the south of the Thames Valley Police area, where Hungerford is situated. In other words, by the time the Tactical Firearms Team had arrived in the market town, Ryan's last shot, apart from the bullet destined to penetrate his own skull, had been fired. The armed response, according to the critics, had quite simply been too late.

That is not to suggest, however, that there was no armed presence before the arrival of the Tactical Firearms Team. Because for almost one hour before the appearance in Hungerford of the specialist squad, officers from the Diplomatic Protection group, who happened to be training nearby, had already made their way to the market town. Though no match for Ryan's armoury, they too were in possession of weapons. But lacking reliable information as to the gunman's precise whereabouts, they managed only to contain the area where he had last been seen. In fact Ryan had long since moved on, and was instead stalking the streets of Hungerford, picking off passers by as he went.

There were others who also perceived the role of these particular officers to be both weak and ineffectual. Even Major John Hathway, himself a former Mayor of Hungerford, felt compelled to speak out in the television programme in which Colin

Greenwood appeared: 'It was very unlike a military operation. The police seemed to me to be too keen on finding out where Ryan was before they deployed their troop. Under military conditions I suspect that we would have gone forward to try and come in contact with the enemy. After all, it was known that it was only one man. There was a small party, admittedly, who moved forward across the Common and deployed. But they only went about 150 yards before taking up a position of cover. From there they just looked on in the general direction of where they thought he was.'

Chief Inspector Glyn Lambert, who headed the Tactical Firearms Team that day, is quick to repudiate the notion that members of his unit should have been dispatched to Hungerford any earlier. For although some fifteen of his men had been ready to go into action, he had decided to wait a few minutes longer until the whole team had assembled.

'They arrived as an organized package and were armed and deployed, rather than arriving piecemeal, ill-equipped and disorganized,' Chief Inspector Lambert explained to lawyers representing a number of victims' families at the inquest. 'That is the system that Thames Valley Police operates. And the system on this occasion worked properly. As for those officers from the [Diplomatic] Protection group, they didn't move from their position at Hungerford Common because they quite simply had nowhere to go. People have asked why they didn't move across the Common, to which I say, move where?'

Charles Pollard, the Assistant Chief Constable of the Thames Valley Police, was not at all happy when he viewed the hour-long *This Week* Special. His force had co-operated with the television programme's makers, even allowing them to have exclusive access to police tapes recorded as the incident was unfolding, on the grounds that the public had a right to know.

'It's not that we in the police force can't take criticism. We can,' he explains. 'And it is of course right that the role of the police should be closely scrutinized — not just in relation to Hungerford, but in all areas of our work. But that programme was a piece of biased reporting. In fact many people phoned in afterwards to say that they thought it was absolutely disgraceful. I happened to know, for example, that the programme makers were speaking to people from overseas who had experience in this type of incident, and when they refused to be critical of Thames Valley Police, they were edited out of the programme. Because that would have spoiled their line.'

Certainly the coroner at the inquest largely exonerated the Thames Valley Police. Summing up before the jury retired to consider their verdict, Charles Hoile reminded the six women and five men considering the case of the extremely delicate balance which had to be struck. There was an inherent conflict, he explained, between the desire to retain an unarmed police force on the one hand and the easy and early availability of arms on the other.

'So far as the police response is concerned,' the coroner told the jury, 'leaving aside the armed branch of the Force or that part of the Force which can become armed, the response of the police obviously was pretty prompt because quite clearly one of the first people to be killed was PC Brereton answering the call. And he was not alone — he was with another officer in another vehicle and two other officers who were local policemen called to the emergency. Looking at it from that view their response would be difficult to fault. There is then a gap — because the whole character of the occurrence changes from being that of a domestic quarrel to something which is absolutely unprecedented, a man going berserk and killing.'

The jury did not take long to return verdicts of unlawful killing. Nor did they seek to criticize the police. On the contrary, they went out of their way to commend a number of officers, including Constables Brereton, Wood and Maggs and Sergeant Jeremy Ryan. They made only one recommendation to the coroner, which he accepted unconditionally. Speaking at the end of the four-day inquest, Anthony Bridge, the jury foreman, issued a short statement: 'The Jury do feel that semi-automatic weapons should not generally be available and that an individual should not be allowed to own an unlimited quantity of arms and ammunition. However, knowing that this subject is under review by the Government, the Jury makes no detailed recommendations.'

One Bloody Afternoon

The jury foreman was right. The subject of the country's gun laws had indeed moved high on to the political agenda within a few hours of the massacre. Before long Douglas Hurd's Firearms (Amendment) Bill was making rapid progress through its various parliamentary stages, its proposals largely welcomed across the political divide. It came as no surprise that possession of the Kalashnikov assault rifle was to be outlawed forthwith. But the fact was that Ryan killed as many people with his Beretta semi-automatic pistol, and there were no plans to ban that. For, as the Home Secretary explained to the House of Commons at the time, there was only so much the law could do: 'It cannot guarantee against criminal behaviour. Nor can it protect us against the individual who, having complied with all the requirements, loses control in a fit of madness. All we can seek to do is to reduce the risk.'

Would arming the police, or making firearms more easily available to them, further reduce the risk? Despite the experience of Hungerford, the police view remains firmly in favour of retaining an unarmed police force. Even PC Trevor Wainwright, the local policeman whose father was murdered by Ryan, remains convinced that the British bobby should not be seen to be brandishing weapons: 'God forbid that anything like this should ever happen again in any town in England. But if it did, I don't think things would change at all. It would still take some time to get armed units to the scene of any shooting. It's perhaps the price that we have to pay for the policing we expect. Nobody wants to see armed policemen walking down the streets of our towns.'

When it comes to the use of firearms, then, it is almost impossible for the police to please all parties. When a gunman had been on the loose in a quiet country town, they were criticized in some quarters for not having cornered and killed him quickly enough. And yet the previous year, each time the police had responded more speedily, shooting and killing a number of gunmen, there had been an immediate furore. Surely, a number of people had pointed out, such an approach was wholly alien to the long traditions of policing the British Isles. In any case, Mr Charles McLachlan, Her Majesty's Inspector of Constabulary, was soon able to confirm in his official report that arming the police could not be relied on to prevent any such similar shootings in the future.

It is a view with which Chief Constable Charles Pollard, as he now is, heartily concurs. In fact, he goes on to argue that making weaponry more easily available to more local officers — in effect a policy of guns in cars — would be entirely counterproductive: 'The more you have policemen being armed, the more you'll get mistakes. This is precisely what happened in Italy about fifteen years ago. They changed the law to make it easier for the police to have access to arms, and since then they have had about 150 innocent deaths, and 235 people injured. I think that shows very clearly the side of the equation which we need to take into account. It's not that it's just a quaint tradition of ours to be unarmed — it actually means much more effective policing as a whole.'

In his report on the massacre, the Chief Constable was at pains to highlight a number of factors which hampered the police operation. A combination of obsolete and inadequate communications equipment and limited manpower had severely hindered police efforts to contain Ryan. 'However,' he insisted, 'no force, even with the most up-to-date equipment, would have been able to handle the vast flood of varied information coming in during the early stages, particularly up to the last murder being committed.'

Marlyne Vardy and Elizabeth Playle, both of whom lost their husbands in the shootings, were not at all satisfied with the outcome of the various investigations into the police's handling of the massacre. Why, for example, had there not been a public enquiry? The nub of their contention was hardly complex: instead of being diverted away from the massacre, as manifestly ought to have been the case, the police had inadvertently sent the women's husbands directly towards the killing zone and thus to their deaths. Did this not constitute an appalling example of gross incompetence on the part of the police? Their formal complaints were duly investigated by an outside force, but a police force nonetheless — the Hampshire Constabulary — under the supervision of the Police Complaints Authority. But no action was taken against those officers who had allowed Eric Vardy and Ian Playle to proceed into Hungerford. For the two widows, it served only to add a legacy of anger and bitterness to their feelings of total loss and grief. 'All I ever wanted,' Elizabeth Playle would later lament, 'was an apology. Just for someone from the police to say sorry. But I didn't even get that.'

Her Majesty's Inspector of Constabulary made no specific criticisms of the Thames Valley Police in relation to their handling of the massacre. But neither did he seek to praise their operation. He confined himself instead to making recommendations, his report containing sixty-one suggestions for reform, covering a wide variety of issues of policing. Many of his recommendations have since been implemented. And many have been summarily ignored.

'In our debriefs we have been through it countless times,' Chief Inspector Lambert explains. 'Could we have saved more lives? Could we have got there quicker? Could we have been more professional and deployed more quickly? Well, with the benefit of hindsight, of course, we would have done certain things differently. But if I am asked would we have acted any differently in terms of our overall approach, I think that the answer is no. We did locate Ryan; we did contain the school. I don't think that more lives could have been saved. Containing a deranged gunman is a very difficult thing to do. Just imagine someone appearing right now, wherever you are, and that person starting to go mad with a powerful weapon — how long would it be before armed police could successfully contain him? It's not easy.'

The car in which Kathleen Wainwright was travelling might also have proceeded in a different direction had the roadblocks established in Hungerford been operating more effectively that day. But they were not. And her husband, Douglas, was killed as a consequence of that. Nonetheless, Kathleen Wainwright has steadfastly refused to condemn the police: 'There's only one person I blame for what happened to my husband. And that's Michael Ryan. We can all say things after the event, what they should have done and so on. But who would have dreamed a thing like this was ever going to happen in a lovely little town like Hungerford? Nobody was prepared for it. We weren't prepared for it. The police weren't prepared for it. They did their best.'

Chief Inspector Laurie Fray, who was at the time in charge of the police press office, is satisfied that the tightening of the firearms law and licensing procedures which has taken place as a result of Hungerford has succeeded in striking a satisfactory balance: 'I think that it's probably about right now. But at the end of the day you can't legislate against nutters. It would be just as possible for someone to kill sixteen people by putting a concrete slab on a railway line. And you can't then outlaw concrete slabs.'

Chief Constable Charles Pollard puts the vexed question of the police response to Hungerford rather differently: 'Many of my officers showed extreme bravery at Hungerford. It was precisely because of good policing that a quite impossible situation was successfully resolved. It was damn good policing. I know it took a long time. But I don't think people appreciate how it might have been. Let's look at it another way. Had we not shown the caution we did, it is entirely within the bounds of possibility that four or five members of the Tactical Firearms Team could have been picked off by Ryan on the loose with his Kalashnikov. If not even more. Then people would have been pointing the finger at me — and quite rightly so. They would have said: "You allowed your men to go in like that? You must have been stark raving mad."'

On 25 August 1987, just six days after the massacre, Ron Tarry was asked to travel to London to participate in Nick Ross's BBC Radio 4 phone-in. He was particularly anxious to appeal to listeners to stay away from Hungerford. 'We want to cleanse ourselves of this. It is time for the people of Hungerford to comfort and help each other,' he said.

Ron Tarry had barely finished broadcasting his heartfelt appeal when a middle-aged man, prepared to identify himself only as 'John from Hertfordshire', called in to warn that he considered himself to be a potential Michael Ryan. His weapon was not a Kalashnikov but a crossbow. He had been influenced not by the film *Rambo* but a book by Colin Wilson entitled *The Outsider*. 'There is more than one Michael Ryan about,' said the caller. 'I am also a loner and a perpetual outsider. Nothing can be done to help me. Only recently I bought a crossbow. I keep it locked away, and I don't think I will harm anyone with it. But I have been in and out of institutions. It just amazes me that someone like myself could buy a crossbow with a pull of 125lb, without a licence, for just £135. The thing is, I can act irrationally. My medical history shows that I have done so in the past.'

As Hertfordshire Police set about trying to contact the man, Ron Tarry returned to Hungerford. For the first time since the shootings, the man who had justifiably won acclaim as the 'voice of Hungerford' found himself too shocked to comment. Driving home along the M4, he wondered how many more potential Ryans there are in our midst.

17.
'Our Saviour will
receive him fittingly'

Several years have elapsed since the Hungerford
massacre. But seldom in the Berkshire market town is
the name of Michael Ryan heard. For the people of
Hungerford prefer to allude to the slaughter rather
than to speak about it directly. So there is instead
often a reference to 'the tragedy', 'the events of 19
August' or 'that dreadful day'. A booklet entitled
'Hungerford Remembered', the entire proceeds of
which were donated to the Tragedy Fund, barely
mentioned Ryan's victims, let alone the gunman
himself. Even five years after the massacre, when a
small memorial garden was opened in the town, there
was that same lingering reluctance to mention the

unmentionable: the name of Michael Ryan. Yet his shadow had hovered over that inauguration ceremony, just as it had done at every one of the funerals of his sixteen victims.

Nonetheless, as early as the first anniversary of the massacre the press felt able to report on a community whose wounds were healing rather rapidly. *The Scotsman* ran the headline 'Hungerford learns to smile again', while the *Daily Express* confidently asserted that 'Life starts again in the vale of tears'. This might well have been true for some. But for others it was not. Liz Brereton explains: 'I'm still missing Roger very much. In fact I still love him very much indeed. Someone once told me that I didn't — that I loved only his memory. That's just not true — it's Roger I still love. That doesn't stop me having a go at him, mind you, from time to time. I still talk to his photograph — I keep a rather smiley one of him by the bed. One day I was having a rather hard time and I was sure that his grin was wider than it usually is. I suddenly found myself getting angry at the photograph, shouting out: "And what are you grinning at?" — whereupon I slammed it down. Then I thought, poor old thing, I'm still shouting at him even though he's gone.'

Jenny Barnard, by contrast, had been able to speak about seeing light at the end of the tunnel when she had participated in the BBC's *Everyman* programme, broadcast on the eve of the first anniversary of the massacre. That progress had continued apace, and within fifteen months of the death of her husband, Barney, she married Sam Sanchez, the man who had helped her so much during the earlier stages of her grief. Fists had flown shortly after their wedding ceremony when the bride, dressed in an off-the-shoulder pink dress, lashed out at a local freelance photographer, landing a punch on his cheek. Permanently hounded by the press, Jenny Sanchez longed for the right of privacy to become enshrined in English law.

The memory of Sue Godfrey, the first of the massacre victims, is perpetuated in a rather different way. For shortly after her death, staff at Reading's Battle Hospital — where Sue had worked as a ward sister until the birth of James — raised well over £3,000. This money was put into a special account known as the Susan Godfrey Memorial Fund, and it now provides for the distribution of annual bursaries to Berkshire students or trained nurses to undertake further education or research in a specific field of medicine. Brian Godfrey attended the first ceremony, held at Battle Hospital, in January 1989. It was there that Sister Anne McDonald, one of three recipients of an award, recalled her former care sister's sense of fun and infectious laughter which used regularly to fill the wards.

Several years later, the ramifications of Hungerford continue to manifest themselves, and in a number of different ways. Anne Eggleton, the senior nursing sister in charge of the Accident and Emergency department at the Princess Margaret Hospital in Swindon on the day of the massacre, and whose calm professionalism was praised by doctors and administrators alike, took her own life shortly after the turn of the new year in 1990. Her husband Stephen Eggleton, an ambulanceman who had himself braved Ryan's bullets, found her body in the fume-filled garage of their Swindon home.

Christopher Larkin, a young policeman and one of the first officers on the scene, was honoured as a hero for his courage that August afternoon. He was to lose not his life but his liberty. For he was jailed in 1991 for six years after a trial at Reading Crown Court for having robbed a building society. He had left the police force shortly after the tragedy, turning first to alcohol and then to crime. His sentence was reduced on appeal by Mr Justice Leonard to four years, the Court of Appeal accepting that the police officer had been deeply affected by the massacre.

'My lingering impression,' remembers Ron Tarry, 'even all these years on, is did it really happen here? I myself launched the appeal. I was involved in the whole aftermath of the tragedy and still I ask, can it really have happened here in Hungerford? Did all those people lose their lives — and all for no reason? Even some of those who saw Ryan in the process of gunning people down thought that it must be a film or something — because it all seemed to be unreal. My main reflection, though, is on the terrific response of everyone. I was so gratified and uplifted by the help

that was forthcoming. Of course people knew that
they couldn't bring back people who had died — it
was just an attempt to minimize the suffering. And
that was very rewarding.'

The other key player in the aftermath of the
massacre was undoubtedly the Reverend Salt.
Working closely with the Mayor, he had been a tower
of strength, his deep faith shining through. Some
social workers expressed amazement that the vicar was
not offered counselling by the Church. The truth was
that God had carried him through this difficult time.
Nonetheless, a year after the massacre, after the vicar
had addressed first Oxford's Victim Support Group
and then a group of clergy on the events of 19 August
1987, the traumas of the previous months suddenly
appeared to catch up with him. For no apparent
reason he suddenly developed shingles, although he
had not the slightest doubt that the origins of his
illness were entirely psychosomatic: 'It was like
unburdening myself, I suppose. That once that first
year had passed, it was as if I had permission to relax.
And that was precisely the moment when it all caught
up with me and I was sick for some time. I am sure
that it was in reality all about the tragedy.'

It did not take the Reverend Salt long to recover.
But Liz Brereton still finds it difficult to relax. Like
Jenny Sanchez and Brian Godfrey, she has gone on to
form a new relationship. But, unlike Jenny and Brian,
she continues to feel entirely shackled by the past: 'I
am seeing someone at the moment — but I do find it

very difficult. Because I am still in love with my husband Roger. And therefore this is stopping me from loving that other person. I've tried to explain this, but he finds it very difficult to understand. I compare something awful — which I know I shouldn't do. I also used to feel guilty, because obviously there has been a financial side to it all — a policeman killed on duty and so on — whereas there might be a widow down the road, suffering like me, but who lost her husband through him having, say, a heart attack. So then I've had guilt piled on top of the grief. Fortunately, though, I still do feel that Roger is in the house with me and the boys. He still talks to me. If I am having a bit of an off day, for example if it's Roger's birthday, I'll hear him say: "Come on, girl, pull yourself out of it — have a drink." And then sometimes, out of the corner of my eye, I think I can see something, and therefore that he is here. And then he says: "Get on with your life, girl — I am here waiting for you." '

'I can well appreciate if it's not possible for people like Liz Brereton,' Ron Tarry concludes, 'who are so closely involved in the tragedy, if they do not feel able to forgive Michael Ryan. But I can forgive him. We should always forgive. Not to forget, but to forgive, just as we should forgive other wrong-doings from the past. I know it is difficult, but I do think that it has to be done. I would be the first to admit, though, how hard this process can be when the killings were so random and senseless. All in all, looking back, I can't say that I feel privileged to have been involved. But it was an incredible experience nonetheless. I wish it could have been for a positive or happy reason, but that was not to be. I do feel very honoured indeed, despite that fact, to have played some small part.'

What of Ryan himself? After his suicide at the John O'Gaunt School, tests of all kinds were carried out on his corpse. It was part of a wide-ranging enquiry designed to provide the elusive explanation as to his motives. Perhaps, some people whispered, he had the AIDS virus or hepatitis, or signs of drug abuse or homosexual activity would be found. In fact the only change to his body other than the gunshot wound itself was some fatty change in his liver consistent with mild alcohol abuse. Dr Richard Shepherd, the Home Office pathologist who examined Ryan's body, even went out of his way to see if he might be able to detect some signs, however slight, of disturbance in Ryan's brain. But as with every test carried out, nothing abnormal was found. To everyone's regret, the very best of modern medical science proved wholly unable to provide even the hint of an explanation as to why Ryan had run amok with his lethal armoury. But the completion of these tests had at least meant that arrangements for his funeral could be allowed to proceed.

As Ryan's relatives made contact with a crematorium in Reading, feelings in Hungerford were running rather high as to who should attend his funeral, who should not and indeed where and when it should be held. Someone even wrote to the Mayor asking him to ensure that Ryan be buried at sea and without a single witness, as if Ron Tarry had some say in the matter. In fact it was the Reverend Salt who was to be the main target for attack.

'Some people had a go at me for assisting at Michael Ryan's funeral,' the vicar recalls. 'But to be honest it simply did not cross my mind not to go. In the Church of England, you bury anyone who is within the confines of your parish. You look upon that person as a parishioner whether or not he actually came to your church. I knew very well how angry people were with Michael Ryan. Don't think that I wasn't angry too. I was. But he was a fellow human being made in the image of God. We are all vulnerable as human beings, and whatever our vicissitudes, not to give respect to our human frame — even in terms of burial — denies our humanity. So of course I was there at the end.'

That end was rather bleak and in stark contrast to the crowded funerals of Ryan's victims. For in the middle of the morning of 3 September 1987, fifteen days after the massacre, a lone hearse bearing Ryan's body pulled out of the mortuary of the Royal Berkshire Hospital. Slowly, in a thin drizzle of rain, it made its way through traffic to the West Chapel at Reading Crematorium. There, outside and braving the elements, a large press corps had assembled. There was the usual jockeying for position as photographers vied with one another for the best photographs of

Ryan's coffin. As the four pall-bearers prepared to carry their load, Fred Stannard, a distant relative, stepped forward to place a bouquet of pink and orange gladioli, carnations, tiger lilies and chrysanthemums on top of the coffin. It was one of just two floral tributes.

There were to be no hymns and few words of comfort. Only seven people were to attend the service, due to last a little more than a quarter of an hour. Then, suddenly, security was heightened. An illuminated sign came on, requesting 'Silence Please, Service in Progress'. The funeral of Michael Ryan had begun. Canon John Reynolds conducted the service with the Reverend Salt, but it was the vicar of Hungerford who was to be the more eloquent that day.

'The Prayer Book collect for this week says that we pray to a God who shows Almighty Power "most chiefly in showing mercy and pity". Thank God for that — for all of us need God's mercy and forgiveness. We come now to commit the body and soul of Michael to God's mercy. How sad it all is — we grieve for all those who have suffered and been bereaved in this tragedy. You will feel for them all, and especially the personal loss of Dorothy. Sadder still when we think of Michael — a lost soul who caused the loss of so many loved ones. But God is judge, and we must not take that power into our hands. Only love can overcome, and only love can bring true forgiveness and reconciliation, which we all need. For me, the true depth and concern we should have for one another, and which reflects the compassion of Christ, was written on a scrap of paper and found by the body of a dead child in Ravensbruck concentration camp, where over 92,000 women and children died:

'"Oh Lord, remember not only the men and women of good will, but also those of ill will. But do not only remember all the suffering they have inflicted on us, remember the fruits we brought, thanks to this suffering, our comradeship, our loyalty, our humility, the courage, the generosity, the greatness of heart which has grown out of all this, and when they come to judgement, let all the fruits that we have borne, be their forgiveness!"

'Jesus will judge rightly, because He understands — He is the son of Man.'

The pine coffin containing the body of Michael Ryan then disappeared behind the crematorium's curtains, its moulded plastic handles buckling first in the intense heat and flames. All of the expenses were borne by Ryan's uncle, Stephen Fairbrass.

The following day the tabloid press reported Ryan's funeral in predictable style. Little was heard of the vicar's sermon, which he had written out verbatim, for, with the press hovering, he wanted to be sure of exactly what he said. For the *Daily Mirror* it was 'Gone For ever — Beast Ryan's last exit', while the *Daily Express* insisted that there was 'No Resting Place for Rambo'. The *Daily Star* headlined just three words: 'Fry in Hell.' The *Guardian* spoke not of evil beasts or maniac monsters, but of the meagre cremation service itself. It was, the paper said, 'the hygienic modern counterpart of the burial of a Victorian murderer in a quick-lime grave'.

The greatest press interest, however, was reserved for what was dubbed the riddle of the red roses. In fact there were not just red roses, but ten white ones too, in addition to ten red carnations and a dozen white chrysanthemums, all gathered together with a large and attractive white bow. They had been handed to one of the pall-bearers, Raymond Coates, by an unidentified blonde woman in her twenties, shortly before the funeral had begun. Her only comment had been: 'This is for Michael Ryan', whereupon she had disappeared. It would later emerge that the woman had spent a little under fifteen pounds on the bouquet at a florist's in Chippenham, although no name or message was attached to her bouquet. Since she ensured that she left no clues from which her particulars might later be ascertained, her motives in sending the flowers and indeed her identity remain a mystery.

Shortly after the Hungerford massacre Ryan's burnt-out house was bulldozed. His extensive range of weaponry and arsenal was eventually destroyed by the police, and his prized Vauxhall Astra GTE met a similar fate. After the cremation, his ashes were taken away by relatives and scattered at a secret location. Few traces remain, therefore, to suggest that Britain's worst mass killer had ever existed at all. Other than sixteen gravestones of his victims.

Ron Tarry was not at that funeral. There had never been any question of his attending. But it was not long before the press were knocking on his door asking for a couple of lines. He issued a short statement on behalf of the people of Hungerford: 'The feeling,' he said, 'is one of relief. That the man who has caused so much anguish can now be forgotten. We have our lives to get on with in this town. So it really is the end of a chapter.'

After the cremation, Ryan's relatives emerged with their heads bowed. Hurrying past journalists and television crews, they too wanted to get on with their lives. But they were not to leave without any comment whatsoever. For the one wreath which did bear a message seemed to speak for them all: 'Our Saviour will receive him fittingly.'

ORDER YOUR COPIES OF
TRUE CRIME TITLES DIRECTLY

Name: ....

Address: ....

             ....

             ....

Daytime tel: ....

Card (*tick as appropriate*)

    Visa   ☐   Mastercard ☐

    Access   ☐   Switch   ☐

Card Number: ....

Expiry date: ....

For Switch cards only:

Issue date: ....   Issue number: ....

Please send me (*tick as appropriate*)

☐ *Deadlier than the Male* Wensley Clarkson

☐ *Natural Born Killers* Kate Kray

☐ *In the Company of Killers* Norman Parker

☐ *The Spanish Connection* John Lightfoot

☐ *Doctors Who Kill* Wensley Clarkson

☐ *Deadly Affair* Nicholas Davies

☐ *Female of the Species* Wensley Clarkson

☐ *Women in Chains* Wensley Clarkson

☐ *The Murder of Rachel Nickell* Mike Fielder

☐ *Vigilante!* Ron Farebrother and Mark Short

☐ *Caged Heat* Wensley Clarkson

☐ *Sunday Bloody Sunday* Drew Mackenzie

☐ *Brothers in Blood* Tim Brown and Paul Cheston

All titles are £4.99. Postage and packing are free.